THE LONDONERS &
THE GREEN CARNATION

Borgo Press Books by FRANK J. MORLOCK

The Chevalier d'Éon and Other Short Farces (Editor)
Chuzzlewit
Congreve's Comedy of Manners
Crime and Punishment
Cyrano and Molière: Five Plays by or About Molière (Editor)
Falstaff (with William Shakespeare, John Dennis, and William Kendrick)
Fathers and Sons
The Idiot
Isle of Slaves and Other Plays (Editor)
Jurgen
Justine
The Londoners & The Green Carnation: Two Plays
Lord Jim
The Madwoman of Beresina and Other Napoleonic Plays (Editor)
Notes from the Underground
Oblomov
Old Creole Days
Outrageous Women: Lady Macbeth and Other French Plays (Editor)
Peter and Alexis
The Princess Casamassima
A Raw Youth
The Stendhal Hamlet Scenarios and Other Shakespearean Shorts from the French (Editor)
Two Voltairean Plays: The Triumvirate; and, Comedy at Ferney (editor)
The Widow's Husband; and, Porthos in Search of an Outfit: Two Dumasian Comedies (Editor)
Zeneida & The Follies of Love & The Cat Who Changed into a Woman: Two Plays (Editor)

THE LONDONERS & THE GREEN CARNATION

TWO PLAYS ADAPTED FROM THE
NOVELS OF ROBERT HICHENS

FRANK J. MORLOCK

THE BORGO PRESS
MMXIII

THE LONDONERS & THE GREEN CARNATION

Copyright © 2013 by Frank J. Morlock

FIRST EDITION

Published by Wildside Press LLC

www.wildsidebooks.com

DEDICATION

For my dear friends,
Jane Eaton and Ron Landers

CONTENTS

THE LONDONERS 9
CAST OF CHARACTERS. 10
ACT I, Scene 1 12
ACT II, Scene 2. 56
ACT II, Scene 3. 93
ACT III, Scene 4 98
ACT III, Scene 5 113
ACT III, Scene 6 120
ACT IV, Scene 7 130
ACT V, Scene 8. 161
THE GREEN CARNATION. 185
CAST OF CHARACTERS. 186
SCENE I 187
SCENE II. 207
SCENE III 218
SCENE IV 221
ABOUT THE AUTHOR 225

THE LONDONERS
A PLAY IN FIVE ACTS

CAST OF CHARACTERS

Mrs. Verulam

Marriner, Mrs. Verulam's maid

Mrs. Van Adam

Mrs. Verulam's butler

Mr. Hyacinth Rodney

Bun Emperor (Mr. Lite)

Empress (Mrs. Lite)

Harrison, the Empress' butler

Mr. James Bush

Mr. Ingerstall

Duchess

Duke

Lady Pearl

Mr. Bliggins

Jacob Minnindick

ACT I
SCENE 1

A drawing room in Mrs. Verulam's mansion in London, in the 1890s.

Mrs. Verulam

Oh, Marriner! Oh, Marriner—how terribly hot it is.

Marriner

The heat is severe, ma'am, for this season of the year.

Mrs. Verulam

I am as pale as Pierrot.

Marriner

I beg pardon, ma'am?

Mrs. Verulam

Pierrot, Marriner, is the legendary emblem of—but it is too hot for history. (spying roses)

What is all that?

Marriner

From Mr. Hyacinth Rodney, ma'am. They are remarkably fine specimens, ma'am. I often think—

Mrs. Verulam

Yes, Marriner, what do you think?

Marriner

That we are like flowers, ma'am. We fade and die so soon.

Mrs. Verulam

Dear me, Marriner, what original thoughts you have.

Marriner

I can't help them coming, ma'am. They seem to take me like a storm, ma'am.

Mrs. Verulam (examining a tray of cards)

Oh, more cards. What curious names people are born with! Why will so may people call?

Marriner

I think they wish to see you, ma'am.

Mrs. Verulam (glumly)

That is the problem.

Marriner

I love problems, ma'am.

Mrs. Verulam

Then solve this one. Why do people with immortal souls spend their lives leaving tiny oblong cards on other people with immortal souls—whom they scarcely know, and don't care a straw about? Why do they do it, Marriner?

Marriner

Might I speak, ma'am?

Mrs. Verulam

I ask you to.

Marriner

I don't feel convinced their souls are immortal, ma'am. I have my doubts, ma'am.

Mrs. Verulam

You're certainly in fashion. But, what makes it all the more strange—if we have only one life, why should we waste it in leaving cards?

Marriner

Very true, ma'am.

Mrs. Verulam (rising dramatically from her seat)

Marriner, we are fools! That is why we do it. That is why we do a thousand things that bore us—and other people. Give me all those notes.

(Marriner brings the notes.)

Mrs. Verulam (after opening several)

Oh, I can't open anymore! Heavens! Are we human, Marriner? Are we thinking, sentient beings, that we live this life of absurdity? Thus do we deliberately complicate our existence—already so complicated, whether we will or no. Ah, it is intolerable. The season is a disease. London is a vast lunatic asylum.

Marriner

Oh, ma'am!

Mrs. Verulam

And we, who call ourselves civilized, are the incurable patients. Give me something to read. Let me try to forget where I am and what I am.

(Marriner brings a journal.)

Mrs. Verulam

Marriner, why do you give me this to read?

Marriner

I thought you had not seen it, ma'am.

Mrs. Verulam

Leave me, Marriner.

(Marriner curtsies and exits.)

Mrs. Verulam (turning to her squirrel in its cage)

Tommy, listen to me. Do you know that you are like me? Do you know that I, too, am in a cage, that I, too, am revolving in a prison, where everything must go round and round? I am so tired of it, Tommy, so tired of my cage—and yet, do you know, half the world is trying to get into it? And cannot! Isn't that absurd?

(Reenter Marriner, followed by Mrs. Van Adam.)

Marriner

Mrs. Van Adam!

Mrs. Verulam

Dearest Chloe!

Mrs. Van Adam

Darling Daisy!

Mrs. Verulam

Marriner, say—not at home—this afternoon..

Marriner

Yes, ma'am.

(exits)

Mrs. Verulam

Oh, Chloe—But, why is your hair cut so short?

Mrs. Van Adam

Oh, it is so hot in Florida that I wanted to have as little about me as possible.

Mrs. Verulam

It makes you look just like a man!

Mrs. Van Adam

I'll grow it again.

Mrs. Verulam

Have you brought a maid?

Mrs. Van Adam

No.

Mrs. Verulam (indicating a seat beside her)

Come and sit down. It's so strange for us to be together again. How many years is it?

Mrs. Van Adam

And now, you're a widow and the darling of London!

Mrs. Verulam

And you— By the way, how is Mr. Van Adam?

Mrs. Van Adam

I am told he is quite well.

Mrs. Verulam

You are told! You are told!

Mrs. Van Adam

Your house is delicious! Florida is lonely. It was cool of me to cable you I was coming. But, you don't mind?

Mrs. Verulam

I am delighted. I've been wanting you to come for so long.

Mrs. Van Adam

And the season is just beginning?

Mrs. Verulam (sighing)

Yes. It's just beginning.

Mrs. Van Adam

It's perfect.

Mrs. Verulam

Chloe, when I was in Paris, I was a little fool.

Mrs. Van Adam

You think I'm still pretty, don't you?

Mrs. Verulam

Lovely, with that short hair.

Mrs. Van Adam

And immensely rich. Give me London to play with.

Mrs. Verulam

But, my dear—

Mrs. Van Adam

Yes. You can do it. You are the pet of society.

Mrs. Verulam

Nonsense.

Mrs. Van Adam

If you only knew how I long to get into it!

Mrs. Verulam

If you only knew how I long to get out of it!

Mrs. Van Adam (looking at the salver)

What a heap of invitations.

Mrs. Verulam (bored)

Today's.

Mrs. Van Adam

May I look at them?

Mrs. Verulam

If you like. They're stupid.

Mrs. Van Adam

Stupid! To have the honor to meet the Prince and Princess of—(hugging her) Oh, you darling! Take me with you—oh, do take me with you.

Mrs. Verulam

Where?

Mrs. Van Adam

To see the Prince and the Princess.

Mrs. Verulam

You will find it terribly dull.

Mrs. Van Adam

Dull? Never!

Mrs. Verulam

You don't understand things. You don't know what London society is for a woman.

Mrs. Van Adam (rapturously)

Heaven!

Mrs. Verulam

Purgatory. We have to talk when we have nothing to say. We have to be made love to—

Mrs. Van Adam (delighted)

Ahh—

Mrs. Verulam

Eat when we are not hungry. Stand like sheep in a pen for hours at a stretch.

Mrs. Van Adam

Yes, but the other sheep!

Mrs. Verulam

All sheep baa in the same way.

Mrs. Van Adam

Mercy, darling! You a farmer!

Mrs. Verulam

No. It was James Bush who taught me all about sheep.

Mrs. Van Adam

James Bush?

Mrs. Verulam

Yes.

Mrs. Van Adam

Is Mr. Bush in society?

Mrs. Verulam

He? Never!

Mrs. Van Adam

Oh, then, don't let's talk about him anymore.

Mrs. Verulam

All right. But, you must know I have come to a great resolution.

Mrs. Van Adam

What is it?

Mrs. Verulam

That this season is my last. I intend to leave town by the first of July.

Mrs. Van Adam

The first of July. Oh, by that time, I shall know everybody, and—

Mrs. Verulam

Be as weary as I am.

Mrs. Van Adam

Be able to manage for myself. Besides, darling, society won't let you leave it.

Mrs. Verulam

That's the terror which pursues me night and day. I have made many attempts. Once, I lost all my fortune—

Mrs. Van Adam

What?

Mrs. Verulam

Gave out that I had, you know.

Mrs. Van Adam

And, what happened?

Mrs. Verulam

It was dreadful. Everybody rallied round me. Have you ever been rallied round?

Mrs. Van Adam

Never.

Mrs. Verulam

It's most fatiguing. It's worse than the Derby. I believe there's only one way in which I could do it.

Mrs. Van Adam

What way is that?

Mrs. Verulam

Compromise myself seriously.

Mrs. Van Adam

How?

Mrs. Verulam

I could be divorced.

Mrs. Van Adam

Divorced! Would that help you much?

Mrs. Verulam

Oh, it would save me. I should be out of everything! Alas, I was born respectable. And besides, my husband is dead, so I cannot divorce. But, tell me about Mr. Van Adam. Why isn't he with you?

Mrs. Van Adam (evasively)

Well, you see his oranges—

Mrs. Verulam

Oranges?

Mrs. Van Adam (hurriedly)

Yes, he grows them on a gigantic scale, and they can't be left.

Mrs. Verulam

Chloe, remember, we were in school together.

Mrs. Van Adam (brazening it out)

But, it is true. Oranges require a great deal of looking after.

Mrs. Verulam

Oh, well, if you prefer to keep me I the dark, I won't say another word.

Mrs. Van Adam (owning up)

You're right. It's not the oranges.

Mrs. Verulam

Of course not.

Mrs. Van Adam

Mr. Van Adam and I have parted.

Mrs. Verulam

Parted!

Mrs. Van Adam

We are separated.

Mrs. Verulam

Legally?

Mrs. Van Adam

Divorced, actually.

Mrs. Verulam

You divorced him already?

Mrs. Van Adam

How rapidly you jump to conclusions.

Mrs. Verulam

Jump! But—

Mrs. Van Adam

I did not say I divorced him. Now, did I? Did I? Oh, I do dislike these implications.

Mrs. Verulam

I hope HE divorced you for something—American.

Mrs. Van Adam

Now, what do you mean?

Mrs. Verulam

Oh, disliking Thanksgiving, or clams, incompatibility I think you call it.

Mrs. Van Adam

No, it was an English action I was divorced for.

Mrs. Verulam

Than, it was for something—bad?

Mrs. Van Adam (hotly)

No, not at all! He is one of those men with a temperament—if he loves you—and he did love me.

Mrs. Verulam

A temperament! Now, please, don't abuse a man for being deformed. I'm afraid you've done something dreadful.

Mrs. Van Adam

No, no. At first, we were fashionably unhappy together. I liked his fury, but there was no variety in him at all. And, one does look for variety in a man.

Mrs. Verulam

Or, in other men.

Mrs. Van Adam

When we were in New York, it was all right. I like a man angry in public. It shows he's really fond of you.

Mrs. Verulam

You always were a bit perverse.

Mrs. Van Adam

But then, we went to Florida. And I meant him to be good-tempered, for we were quite alone. But, he couldn't stop.

Mrs. Verulam

Oh, dear.

Mrs. Van Adam

Then, B. B. Rockmetteller came to visit.

Mrs. Verulam

B. B. Rockmetteller?

Mrs. Van Adam

His dearest chum. He was to sympathize with my husband. That's why he was invited. But, as soon as he arrived, my husband became furiously jealous of him. And then, Huskinson, that's my husband, attacked B. B.— It was my duty to say B. B. was harmless.

Mrs. Verulam

Certainly.

Mrs. Van Adam

But my doing so brought him to the verge of madness. Huskinson went away for a week.

Mrs. Verulam

Leaving B. B.?

Mrs. Van Adam

Yes. And then he came back, and said we had deceived him while he was away.

Mrs. Verulam

How unreasonable! If he hadn't meant you to deceive him, he shouldn't have gone.

Mrs. Van Adam

While B. B. was in the billiard room arguing with my husband, I was locking up the revolvers and packing my trunks. So, I went off. Next thing I knew, he was suing me for divorce.

Mrs. Verulam

Dreadful!

Mrs. Van Adam

Why dreadful? It was all done very quietly. Nobody will hear of it over this way. Besides, I am innocent.

Mrs. Verulam

Then, why didn't you defend it?

Mrs. Van Adam

Because I was in the right!

Mrs. Verulam (agreeably)

Of course.

Mrs. Van Adam (picking up the paper and starting to read it)

Ah, this is your great paper! I want to see my name in it some day. (reading, shocked) Yoiks—I do!

Mrs. Verulam

What is the matter? Are you ill?

Mrs. Van Adam (reading aloud)

A considerable sensation has been caused in Florida, by the Van Adam divorce—etc.—etc.—which caused him to condemn not only his wife, but his trusted friend—

Mrs. Verulam (grabbing the paper and reading)

Dearest, you can never get into the cage now.

Mrs. Van Adam (bursting into tears)

Is it quite impossible?

Mrs. Verulam

Quite. If you were a man, that paragraph would open doors for you.

Mrs. Van Adam

Oh, why am I not a man?

Mrs. Verulam

Marriner, my maid—she's marvelously well-informed about everything. Marriner might know. I cannot tell.

Mrs. Van Adam

And, I used to be a man.

Mrs. Verulam

Chloe, dear, collect yourself. Don't deceive yourself for a moment. You have always been what you are now—a woman.

Mrs. Van Adam (doggedly)

No, on. Everybody said so.

Mrs. Verulam

I think you had better lie down quietly.

Mrs. Van Adam

It was at a masquerade ball. I dressed in a tweed suit. I still have it. It reminds me of happy days.

Mrs. Verulam

I'm afraid you love B. B.—I mean your husband.

Mrs. Van Adam

No, no.

Mrs. Verulam

You should have come over as a man, dear. Then London would have been at your feet.

Mrs. Van Adam

Suppose I should? Are you at home this afternoon?

Mrs. Verulam

No, not to anyone.

Mrs. Van Adam

Good. Let me go upstairs and change. Then, I want to talk to you ever so much. Oh, that horrible, wicked paragraph.

(Mrs. Verulam rings a bell and Marriner enters.)

Mrs. Verulam

Marriner, this is Mrs. Van Adam. I want you to take great care of her.

Marriner (to Mrs. Van Adam)

I trust the oranges are doing well, ma'am?

Mrs. Verulam

Marriner will show you to your room, dear.

(Exit Marriner with Mrs. Van Adam.)

Mrs. Verulam

Providence has at last heard my cry.

(Enter butler.)

Butler

Mr. Hyacinth Rodney.

Mrs. Verulam (a little puzzled, since she gave orders she was not at home)

But—

(Enter Mr. Rodney.)

Mrs. Verulam

Thank you for your roses, a thousand times.

Rodney

I did not come to be thanked for giving anyone pleasure. I come to bring glad tidings.

Mrs. Verulam

I shall think of you as a herald angel.

Rodney

Flying ever to my heaven.

Mrs. Verulam (a little uneasy)

But, your tidings?

Rodney

My mission has been successful. The house is yours.

Mrs. Verulam

What house?

Rodney (astonished)

Surely, you have not forgotten that you commissioned me to get you Ribton Marches for the race week?

Mrs. Verulam

Oh, now I remember.

Rodney (pained)

Only now? I opened delicate negotiations weeks ago. One false step would have been instant destruction.

Mrs. Verulam (touched)

My dear Mr. Rodney—

Rodney

Instant destruction! Owing to the temper of the owner, Mr. Lite, the Bun Emperor.

Mrs. Verulam (nonplussed)

The Bun Emperor!

Rodney

So he is known to all the children in the British Isles to whom he caters, as the saying goes.

Mrs. Verulam (not having realized she was dealing with such an exalted personage)

Dear me.

Rodney

Mr. Lite is a man of very peculiar proclivities. I made a minute study of them in order to carry out your instructions.

Mrs. Verulam

It is most good and industrious of you.

(aside)

Whatever shall I do with this house?

Rodney

Oh, I shrink from nothing in such a cause. He's a man of violent temper—devoted to home life and extremely suspicious of strangers.

Mrs. Verulam

What a terrible combination of idiosyncrasies.

Rodney

Precisely. There were moments when despair seized me, and I could have cried aloud like an Eastern Pilgrim—Allah has turned his face from me—

Mrs. Verulam

I am quite ashamed to have given you so much trouble. But, how did you succeed?

Rodney (rising)

Well, I found there was only one string I could play on—his love of titles. I—I ventured to make a promise on your behalf.

Mrs. Verulam

Indeed!

(Mrs. Verulam walks about in agitation.)

Rodney (guiltily)

I said that you would use your influence with Lady Sophia.

Mrs. Verulam

Mamma!

Rodney

With regard to the buns. Did I go too far?

Mrs. Verulam

And, what is poor Mamma to do? I cannot ask her to eat a bun, Rodney, I really can't do that!

Rodney

Such a shocking notion would never have occurred to me. No, no, Lady Sophia must only say a word in praise of his buns.

(pulls out paper)

It reads thus: I beg to say your buns look very inviting, they should be nourishing.

Your influence on the digestion of English children, I feel almost certain, will commend itself to historians of the national diet— Lady Sophia Tree—I think Mr. Disraeli could scarcely improve upon that.

Mrs. Verulam

Mamma has only to sign that?

Rodney

Merely to sign, I assure you.

Mrs. Verulam

Oh, then she will do it. She likes to see herself in print. And, you did this for me?

Rodney (clearing his throat twice and twitching respectfully as if he were about to receive a Knight of the Garter from the Queen)

Yes, ma'am.

(Enter butler.)

Butler

Her Grace the Duchess of Southborough and her daughter.

(Enter the Duchess.)

Duchess

So glad to find you at home. We quite thought you would have been out on such a lovely day.

(butler whispers in her ear)

What do you say—what? Not enough! An extra sixpence? Certainly not! Tell him to go.

(exit Butler)

(resuming, to Mrs. Verulam)

But, I know you are quite independent of weather. In that respect, you are quite like Southborough—he always says—

(Butler reenters and resumes whispering to her)

What? What do you say? He won't go? No, I shan't. Tell him so. Not another penny. We only took him from Whitely's. It isn't more than two miles.

(more whispering)

No, no! Certainly not!

Rodney

Can I be of any service?

Duchess

Oh, thank you, Mr. Rodney. It is only an extortionate cab man. Send him away.

Rodney (going out with butler)

Certainly.

Duchess

Southborough always defies the weather. He is heroic in that regard. He is like—

Rodney (returning)

It is quite right. Lord Birchington is gone.

Duchess

Birchington? You don't mean to tell me the fellow was my brother?

Rodney

Er, yes.

Duchess

Oh, I fancied I knew his face. That quite accounts for the attempt at extortion. Birchington is always in difficulty and I dare say cab driving doesn't pay too well. I hope, I hope, Mr. Rodney, you didn't give in to his demands?

Rodney

Well, really—he seemed so convinced. Just a sixpence, you know.

Duchess

That is the way to become poor, Mr. Rodney. You ought to take more care of your money, and not let my worthless brother prey on you.

Butler (entering)

Mr. Van Adam.

(Enter Mrs. Van Adam, dressed in a tweed suit.)

Mrs. Van Adam (aside to Mrs. Verulam)

Introduce me as my husband.

Mrs. Verulam

The Duchess of Southborough—Mr. Van Adam.

Rodney

I had no idea, no notion at all, that you knew Mr. Van Adam.

Mrs. Verulam

Oh, yes.

Rodney

Besides, I fully understood he was in Florida.

Mrs. Verulam

That makes that paragraph in the—world—all wrong.

Rodney

I wrote it.

Mrs. Verulam (frightened)

You!

Van Adam

An invitation lured me from my orange groves.

Duchess

Oh, then you are staying with Mrs. Verulam?

Van Adam

Yes.

Mrs. Verulam

Oh, yes.

(feebly)

Oh, yes, yes.

Duchess (in a hard voice)

Might I ask for a cup of tea, Mrs. Verulam?

Mrs. Verulam (uneasily)

Certainly. (pouring tea carefully, but putting in fifteen lumps of sugar) You don't take tea with sugar, I think?

Duchess (speaking to Mr. Van Adam)

Gouty? Ah, you and Pearl would sympathize. Let me introduce you to my daughter. Mr. Van Adam—Lady Pearl McAndrew.

Van Adam (bowing)

Charmed.

Pearl

I am not gouty, mother, I am only melancholy. And that is because I cannot, I will not blind myself to the actual condition of the world around me.

Duchess

Oh, my dear, Carlsbad would cure you. (to Mr. Van Adam) But, unfortunately, I cannot afford to send her there just at present.

Rodney

I believe that in the climate of Florida gout is practically unknown. My friend Lord Bernard Roche, Lord Bernard Roche, now in New York City, tells me so.

Van Adam

Oh, yes. Lord Bernard, oh yes, certainly.

Rodney

Lord Bernard is a man to go confidently into any trouble.

Van Adam

Oh, certainly. Most undoubtedly, yes.

Duchess

But, in London, you must forget all your troubles. London is the most cheerful place imaginable.

Pearl (distraught)

Oh, mother!

Duchess

Yes, Pearl, for a healthy person. No doubt you are staying for the season.

Van Adam (after looking at Mrs. Verulam)

Yes.

Duchess

Well, then, you will soon be quite cheerful again. I'd warrant you have been over before, I suppose.

Van Adam

Paris, not London.

Pearl

London is horrible. The Bois de Boulogne makes me sick.

(Enter butler)

Butler

Mr. Ingerstall.

Ingerstall (entering on Pearl's last line)

Paris is the only place in the world.

Pearl

Really!

Ingerstall (getting tea from Mrs. Verulam)

Really. There is no art except in Paris. No possibility of dining out of Paris. No good dressmaker beyond the limits of Paris. No perfect language except the perfect language of Paris. No gaiety, no verve, no acting, no dancing, no love-making worthy of the name, except in Paris.

Duchess

Then, Mr. Ingerstall, why on earth do you always live in London?

Ingerstall

Because I find more caricatures here.

(to Mrs. Verulam)

Please introduce me to that gentleman.

Mrs. Verulam

Mr. Ingerstall—Mrs…Mr. Van Adam.

(They bow to each other.)

Ingerstall

You know Paris?

Van Adam

Yes, quite well.

Ingerstall

You agree with me, then?

Van Adam

Certainly.

Ingerstall

There, your Grace, you see: there are others of my opinion.

Duchess

Ah, but Mr. Van Adam doesn't know London yet.

Rodney

Oh, he must.

Ingerstall

Then, I'll show it to him! Oh, I'll show it to him. Oh, I'll show Mr. Adams London!

Rodney

Van Adam.

(Ingerstall looks puzzled at first.)

Ingerstall

Mr. Van Adam, London. Will you come with me?

Van Adam

Thank you very much.

Ingerstall

That's settled then! And then, we'll see, Duchess, whether this gentleman doesn't swear by blessed Paris to the end of his life.

Duchess

Really, Mr. Ingerstall, you ought to go to the morgue instead of heaven when you die!

(turning to Mrs. Verulam)

What are your plans for the season, Mrs. Verulam? Are you going to Ascot?

Mrs. Verulam

I haven't thought much about it yet.

Rodney (sternly)

Mrs. Verulam has secured through me—

Ingerstall

You really ought to run across the Channel to Longchamps for the races—

Duchess (ignoring Ingerstall and addressing Rodney)

Indeed! Which house do you mean?

Rodney

Ribton Marches.

Duchess

The Bun Emperor's palace! Mrs. Verulam, you are a public benefactor. Is Mr. Van Adam to be of your party?

Mrs. Verulam (helplessly)

Yes.

Duchess

Ribton Marches is a palace. It would hold a regiment.

Rodney

Oh, I scarcely thing Mr. Lite would care to entertain a—

Duchess

I know Mr. Lite very well—a most worthy generous man. He has given me thousands of buns.

Ingerstall (maliciously)

Does your Grace eat so many? If you want a really perfect bun, go to the maison—

Duchess (sharply)

For the poor children. All we have had to do is let the good man use our name in his advertising. Have you made up your house party yet?

Mrs. Verulam

Not yet. The house is—

Duchess

A palace.

Mrs. Verulam

—scarcely settled yet.

Rodney

I'll settle it tonight!

Duchess

If your party is not made up, Mrs. Verulam, I am sure the Duke and I and Lady Pearl will be most happy to join it.

Pearl

Indeed, mother, I do not wish—

Duchess

My dear, nonsense; it will do your gout a deal of good, breathing pine-laden air—if Mrs. Verulam can find room for you.

Mrs. Verulam

I shall be delighted.

Duchess

Then that is settled.

(rising)

It will be an advantage to you to have me at Ribton Marches, because I know all the ins and outs of the place. Well, really, we must be getting on. Come, Pearl.

Pearl (rising and winking at Mr. Van Adam)

Come and see us.

Mrs. Van Adam

Many thanks.

Pearl

Come tomorrow. Mrs. Verulam will give you our address.

Van Adam

With pleasure.

Pearl

Goodbye, Mr. Ingerstall. Perhaps you won't mind just coming out with us to hail a cab?

(Ingerstall rises. Exit Pearl and the Duchess.)

Ingerstall (to Mrs. Van Adam)

I'll come tomorrow morning to show you London.

(exiting)

Mrs. Verulam (hoping to get rid of Mr. Rodney)

You mustn't forget your engagement, Mr. Rodney.

Rodney

I am not likely to forget any detail of my service to you. But we do not dine till half past eight.

Mrs. Verulam

The trains are slow on your line, I believe.

Rodney

Still, they do not take three hours to do six miles.

Mrs. Verulam (closing her eyes and whispering)

The Lord is my shepherd, I shall not want—

Rodney (craftily)

I have heard much of you, Mr. Van Adam.

Van Adam

Indeed?

Rodney

Yes, I have even had the pleasure of writing a little word about you.

Van Adam

May I ask where?

Rodney (tapping the paper)

Here.

Van Adam

Indeed!

Mrs. Verulam

He maketh me to lie down in green pastures—

Rodney

May I have the pleasure of showing you. You will notice a slight mistake at the close. It would not have crept in had I known that we were to have the unexpected pleasure of welcoming you to London. I shall be glad to rectify my error next week.

Van Adam

I am obliged to you.

Rodney

In the meanwhile, anything I can do to render your short stay among us agreeable, I shall be only too happy—

Mrs. Verulam

My cup runneth over.

Rodney

Mitching Dean, my home, is entirely at your disposal. Mitching Dean has an admirable rose garden.

Van Adam

Roses! Ah, English roses are exquisite. I have some dark red ones in my room here.

Rodney

Dark red roses—in your room?

(surveying the room, then turning to Mrs. Verulam in horror)

My train! I must catch it! I must go! I must indeed!

(low to Mrs. Verulam)

Betrayer! Traitress!

(aloud)

My train! Goodbye.

(Mr. Rodney exits hurriedly in some disorder. After a moment Mrs. Van Adam bursts into tears and Mrs. Verulam into laughter. They are both in hysterics.)

Mrs. Verulam

Chloe!

Mrs. Van Adam

Daisy!

Mrs. Verulam

Oh, oh, oh.

Mrs. Van Adam

Ah, ah, ah.

Mrs. Verulam

Don't, or I shall begin again.

(pause)

But, how could you?

Mrs. Van Adam

But, why did you say nobody would be let in?

Mrs. Verulam

I told Marriner. She must have forgotten to tell James.

Mrs. Van Adam

Oh, Daisy, I wonder if it would be possible—

Mrs. Verulam

No, no!

Mrs. Van Adam

Oh, yes, yes!

Mrs. Verulam

Poor Mr. Rodney. They were his roses I put in your room, Chloe.

Mrs. Van Adam

But Marriner—

Marriner (appearing suddenly)

Yes, ma'am.

Mrs. Van Adam

Marriner will keep the secret.

Marriner

With my very best blood, ma'am! With my very best blood!

CURTAIN

ACT II
SCENE 2

Ribton Marches, the palace of the Bun Emperor. The Emperor follows the Empress in. The Empress is evidently upset and is crying.

Emperor

My dear! My dear!

Empress

What's the good of my dear this and my dear that! It's done and it can't be undone.

Emperor

I can't go back on my word, Henrietta.

Empress

Then, why give it? All for a bit of publicity that won't sell half a million buns.

Emperor

I think you underrate Lady Sophia Tree's influence. She will have very great weight in infant circles.

Empress

Well, even if she sells a million, it ain't worth it!

Emperor

Is not, Henrietta, is not.

Empress

Bother! I said ain't.

Emperor (trying to placate her)

If I had not secured Lady Sophia's endorsement when I had the opportunity, it would have haunted me the rest of my life. Go for the names. That's always been my motto. Go for the names.

Empress

Yes, go for the names—and go out of our home!

Emperor

Don't my dear, don't—

Empress

To be turned out in the streets at this time of our lives! And these Londoners— Oh, what will they do to the place?

(sobbing)

I can't bear it.

Emperor

Do to the place? Let them try it. Mr. Harrison has his orders.

Empress

Orders to do what?

Emperor

Ah, let them try it. Let them only try and they will repent it, Henrietta, to the last day of their lives.

Empress

What are you going to do?

Emperor

My duty!

Empress

What then? These 'ere Londoners ain't coming?

Emperor

Are not, my dear, are not. Yes, come they must. But Mr. Harrison has orders to keep an eye on them—morning, noon, and night.

Empress

Night—what the ladies?

Emperor

Only till they retire, of course. If they damage the bedrooms, they shall answer for it.

Empress

Ah, what a man you are!

Emperor

They shall find out what sort of a man I am if they try their tricks here. If so much as a bit of wood is chipped off, or so much as one parrot is missing, they'll repent it to their lives' end, they will.

Empress

Having it out of them won't make it up to us for all we have to go through.

Emperor (sighing)

It's only for six days.

Empress

It will seem six years. And the cottage. Why was it only made to hold a fisherman?

Emperor

My dear, the house in Camberwell was small.

Empress

And so were we, then. But we're a bit bigger now.

Emperor

I do believe I've been a fool.

Empress

You've never spoken a truer word. All I say is don't let that Mr. Rodney come near me. Do they bring their own linen?

Emperor

I'm afraid that we have to provide everything but the food.

Empress

Oh, Perry, Perry, that it should come to this!

Emperor

Still, Mrs. Verulam is—

Empress (interrupting)

A silly sounding name!

Emperor

She's the one who pays the rent.

Empress

Mr. Van Adam, I call that a low name. I never could abide Bible names. Never trust a man with a Bible name.

Emperor

The Duchess of Southborough.

Empress

She's better.

Emperor

Yes, her Grace does know a good bun.

Empress

Mr. Hyacinth Rodney! Fiddle! Foul breath! Mr. Ingerstall. What do you think of him?

Emperor

Sounds like one of those nasty fellows that go worming themselves about in places where they've no business. He'd better not let Mr. Harrison catch him worming himself about when he's here! Henrietta, even if I have to turn them all out, neck and crop! Mr. James Bush. Bush, James Bush. Well, Henrietta?

Empress

I don't know what to think of it. It's not a name to marry.

Emperor

Is it a name to have in our home? A name to have sleeping in our beds?

Empress

Ah, is it?

Emperor

I have my doubts. Shall we ask Mr. Harrison, my dear? We can always rely on him. He can judge of a name on first hearing.

Empress

We might do worse.

Emperor (calling loudly)

Harrison!

Harrison (the butler enters after a moment)

Yes, sir.

Emperor

Mr. Harrison, I believe you are a man of the world.

Harrison

I am, sir.

Emperor

You can judge of a name at first hearing, I presume?

Harrison

Sir?

Emperor

You can tell what you think about a name the first time you hear it?

Harrison

Oh certainly, sir! Oh, most certainly!

Emperor

Very well then. Now, give me your attention, if you please. I have here the name James Bush. James Bush.

Harrison

Indeed, sir, indeed.

Emperor

Well, Mr. Harrison? Well?

Harrison

Not at all, sir. Oh, dear no; not at all. By no means.

Emperor

And, what do you mean by that, Mr. Harrison?

Harrison

James Bush, sir, oh dear, no, sir! James Bush, not at all, by no means, on no account whatever!

Emperor

There, Henrietta! There! You see what Mr. Harrison thinks of him. A feller like that! A feller like that! Mr. Harrison, we depend upon you entirely in this affair! Keep your eye on him!

Harrison

Sir!

Emperor

I say, keep your eye especially on that feller James Bush.

Harrison

Certainly, sir.

Emperor

Don't let him be too much for you, Mr. Harrison. He may have ways, there's no knowing. But, I hold you responsible.

Harrison

I shall see to him, sir. Depend upon me.

Emperor

We do, don't we, Henrietta?

Empress (sobbing)

Mercy knows, we do.

Harrison

I shall not disappoint you, madame. I shall know how to act.

Emperor

I believe that. And, I may add that, if you should cop— If you should catch this feller James Bush at any of his games—you understand.

Harrison

Certainly, sir.

Emperor

And, if you should be one too many for him, we shall not forget it. You will have no reason to regret hereafter any steps you need to take. You understand?

Harrison

Quite so, sir. I shall take them, sir. You may depend.

Emperor

Mr. Harrison.

Harrison

Sir.

Emperor

Remember, they are not to feed the parrots. On no account are they to tamper with the parrots.

Harrison

Certainly not, sir.

Emperor

If you see any symptom to do anything of that kind, you are to check it, Harrison.

Harrison

If I see any symptom—I am to check it.

Emperor

If a single parrot goes wrong, my wife will hold you responsible, Mr. Harrison. You understand that?

(Harrison bows in affirmation)

The pup we shall take with us, Mr. Harrison.

Harrison

The pup you will take—

Emperor

Don't echo me, Mr. Harrison, don't echo me. I will not allow myself to be echoed.

Harrison

Certainly not, sir. Oh, by no means.

Emperor (seeing a long telescope)

Pack that telescope. With that I shall be able to command a considerable portion of the grounds. If I see anything going on here of which I disapprove, I shall summon you by telephone. You will hold yourself in readiness.

Harrison

I shall, sir.

Emperor

Each morning, you will be round by eight o'clock with your report.

Harrison (pained)

By eight, sir?

Emperor

Well, seven if you prefer it. I shall be up. I shall be ready.

Harrison (eagerly)

Oh, eight will be fine, sir. I shall be round by eight.

Emperor

Be careful to omit nothing from that report. Make it ample. I shall have damages out of these people if they dare exceed in any way—or behave in an unseemly manner. You have your own idea of what is unseemly, Mr. Harrison?

Harrison

Oh, decidedly so, sir.

Emperor

Then, I shall hold you responsible. Henrietta?

Empress

Darling.

Emperor

Are you ready?

Empress (dejected)

Oh, is it time?

Emperor

Mr. Harrison.

Harrison

Sir?

Emperor

Is it time? Have you the paper?

(Harrison nods twice)

Read it out.

Harrison

"Arrivals, Monday, June 10th—at 12:30: Mrs. Verulam, Mr. Rodney, Mr. Van Adam—with Mrs. Marriner, maid. At 3:15: Mr. James Bush."

Emperor

Enough, Mr. Harrison. I give you warning!

Harrison (stupefied)

Give me warning, sir! Am I to go, sir?

(faints)

Emperor

Mr. Harrison! Get up! Get up from the floor, sir. Come, come, Mr. Harrison. Rise. Be a man. A glass of water, my dear.

Empress (runs about and returns with water)

Here.

Emperor

There, there—you're spilling it. You mistook my meaning.

Harrison (weakly)

Sir?

Emperor

I meant that I give you warning that we will hold you responsible for Mr. Bush.

Harrison (recovering)

Oh, certainly, sir! I beg pardon! Oh, by no—by all means.

Emperor

The time has come when we must leave you. We go with breaking hearts.

Empress

We do, we do.

Emperor

Do your duty, but don't be put upon. Don't be a slave.

Harrison

Hear, hear!

Emperor

Mr. Harrison!

Harrison

Sir!

Emperor

Is the pony cart at the door?

Harrison

It is, sir! Oh, most decidedly.

Emperor

Goodbye.

(The Empress faints.)

Emperor

Mr. Harrison.

Harrison

Sir!

Emperor

Help me with the missus. Prepare for the Londoners.

(Lights dim, then go up. The Londoners begin to arrive. Enter Mrs. Van Adam, dressed as a man, with Mr. Rodney, Mrs. Verulam, etc.)

Van Adam

Oh, what an enormous house. We shall be lost in it!

Rodney

I assure you, it is quite cozy.

(Harrison comes forward, observing them like a Bobby guarding against the theft of the crown jewels.)

Harrison

I am Harrison.

Mrs. Verulam

What a very remarkable looking man. He seems anxious. Is he ill?

Rodney

Oh no, I think not. I fancy he superintends the servants.

Van Adam

He appears to me like a detective who hasn't mastered the first principle of his profession.

Rodney (blandly)

And, may I ask what that is?

Van Adam

Not to look like one, old chap.

Parrot Voices

Hallelujah. Polly dreadful drunk. What's o'clock, Polly?

(Sound of corks popping.)

Rodney

Pray, don't be alarmed.

Mrs. Verulam

Is it the same man?

Rodney

No, no. They are only the Bun Emperor's talking parrots.

(Rodney, Mrs. Verulam, and Van Adam exit. After a moment a phone bell rings.)

Harrison (going to the phone)

Yes, sir. Yes, sir.

(pause)

I was in the hall watching—

(pause)

Not much to look at, sir—

(pause)

I didn't take particular notice—

(pause)

Rely on me, sir.

(pause)

The parrots shall not be tampered with.

(pause)

Mr. Bush, sir.

(pause)

I will indeed.

(pause)

He shall not, sir.

(pause)

Oh, most decidedly, sir.

(Reenter Van Adam and Mrs. Verulam.)

Van Adam

Mr. Rodney's getting very officious, almost as bad as that horrid little Mr. Ingerstall. He wants Harry to shave me!

Mrs. Verulam

Don't let him, Chloe. Don't be shaved!

Van Adam

My dear, is it likely? I told him I always did it myself.

Mrs. Verulam

I wonder Mr. Rodney hasn't more tact. I keep forgetting you're a man. When shall I remember?

Van Adam

Perhaps when you get no more invitations.

Mrs. Verulam

The goal is in sight.

Van Adam

Well, you are the most extraordinary creature. Daisy, the Duchess means mischief.

Mrs. Verulam

I know.

Van Adam

I'm surprised she came.

Mrs. Verulam

I'm not. She is a woman of courage and resource. In spite of all, she has hopes for you and Lady Pearl. And besides, she hasn't got another invitation for Ascot.

Van Adam

Lady Pearl is rather a shame. Still, I've cured her of the gout.

Mrs. Verulam

He'll be here soon. I'm so excited.

Van Adam

He! Oh, of course, Mr. Bush. Now, don't spoil everything by flirting with James Bush instead of with me.

Mrs. Verulam

James Bush never flirts. He doesn't know the meaning of the word.

(spying Rodney)

Oh, here you are, Mr. Rodney.

Rodney (suspiciously)

Yes, here I am.

(A loud noise off.)

Rodney

What's all this? What the devil is it all?

Mrs. Verulam

Dear me! Can this be Mr. Bush already?

Rodney

I fancy so.

(Enter Bush.)

Van Adam

By Jove, Bungay Marshes to the front.

Mrs. Verulam

Oh, Mr. Bush, I am so glad to see you. Let me introduce you to Mr. Rodney and Mr. Van Adam. The rest of the party comes later.

Bush (to Harrison, who is peering from behind a plant)

What are you after?

Harrison (emerging)

Oh, nothing, sir, not at all, by no means.

Mrs. Verulam

Really, Mr. Rodney. That man is becoming very unnecessary. Can't you keep him in order?

Rodney

I will endeavor. I will certainly endeavor.

Mrs. Verulam (to Bush)

Would you like to go to your room, or will you rest a little first?

Bush (pointing to a chaise lounge)

I'll rest there. I'll have a lie-down. A good lie-down.

(Bush and Rodney go out.)

Mrs. Verulam (eagerly)

Well, dear, well?

Van Adam

Well—

Mrs. Verulam

Isn't he—simple—straightforward—natural?

Van Adam

Oh, quite, quite natural.

Mrs. Verulam

After all the shams and hypocrisies of society, what a contrast, what a relief!

Van Adam

Yes.

Mrs. Verulam

I knew—

(kissing Van Adam)

—You would agree with me.

Van Adam

Daisy, don't!

Mrs. Verulam

Oh, heavens! Could anyone have seen?

Van Adam

No, it's all right. I believe Mr. Bush is the largest human being I have ever seen.

(Van Adam and Mrs. Verulam exit. After a moment, enter Mr. Ingerstall, the Duchess, the Duke, and Lady Pearl from another direction.)

Ingerstall

I think the French way of doing things is by far the best. A Frenchman marries not with the intent of resigning his freedom, but of gaining it.

Duchess (icily)

The French point of view is scarcely a suitable subject of discussion.

Duke

Gaining his freedom, ha, ha—!

(The Duke and Ingerstall wander out. Lady Pearl retires, leaving the Duchess with Mr. Rodney.)

Duchess (icily)

She has been going too far, Mr. Rodney. She has disgusted London.

Rodney

Disgusted London? Oh, no, impossible!

Duchess

You think nothing could, but you are wrong. There is a limit, even in our world, and she has overstepped it. You will see tomorrow in the Enclosure. Martha Sage intends to cut her.

Rodney

Impossible.

Duchess

Nothing is impossible to Martha Sage. I assure you, it is fact.

Rodney (passionately)

It must be prevented. It must, it shall!

Duchess

I don't see how it can be. You don't know Martha Sage.

Rodney

But, indeed, I do. She has often dandled me in her arms.

Duchess (amazed)

What, recently?

Rodney (distractedly)

Yes, yes. Often.

Duchess

Possibly you may have some influence over her then. And, if what you say is true, I hardly think Martha has the right to take the initiative.

Rodney

When I was a little boy.

Duchess

Oh, that's nothing. She dandled everybody. But she doesn't allow anybody to influence her decisions.

Rodney

Then, Mrs. Verulam must be kept out of the Enclosure. She must and shall!

Duchess

That will only delay the matter. In fact, Mr. Rodney, and this I tell you in the strictest confidence, if I don't observe a very great change in Mrs. Verulam's behavior during this week, I am very much afraid that I shall be obliged to agree with Martha. And now, it is tea time.

(Exit the Duchess and Mr. Rodney. Enter Marriner and Mrs. Verulam from a different direction.)

Marriner

Oh, ma'am!

Mrs. Verulam

Why do you say—oh—Marriner? What should you have to say— Oh about?

Marriner

Many things, ma'am, many things.

Mrs. Verulam

Have many more thoughts taken you like a storm?

Marriner

They have, indeed, ma'am.

Mrs. Verulam

If you think so much, you ought to keep a life boat about you.

Marriner

Might I speak, ma'am?

Mrs. Verulam

You may, certainly.

Marriner

Ma'am, I've heard a dreadful thing.

Mrs. Verulam

Dreadful! What about?

Marriner

About you.

Mrs. Verulam

Who from?

Marriner

From Mrs. Crouch, ma'am, her Grace's woman.

Mrs. Verulam

Indeed.

Marriner

Oh, ma'am, she says, ma'am, that Lady Sage is—

Mrs. Verulam

Don't break down, Marriner.

Marriner

She says that, oh, that Lady Sage is going to have nothing at all to do with you in the Enclosure tomorrow, ma'am. Oh dear, dear me! Oh, ma'am, don't go—don't go there. We should not place ourselves between the feet of our enemies, ma'am; no, no, we should not.

Mrs. Verulam

Dear me—

Marriner

There is worse, ma'am. There is treachery, indeed, and there is treason, ma'am—

Mrs. Verulam

Really, one would think that Guy Fawkes was staying in the house.

Marriner

No, ma'am. Indeed, it is not him.

Mrs. Verulam

Then, who is it?

Marriner

The Duchess.

Mrs. Verulam

Really?

Marriner

And it is all because of Mrs. Van Adam. Oh, do please tell them, ma'am.

(Enter Rodney.)

Rodney

Could I have a word with you?

Mrs. Verulam

Certainly.

(Exit Marriner, weeping.)

Rodney

Where do you think of watching the races tomorrow, may I venture to ask?

Mrs. Verulam

The Enclosure, of course.

Rodney

Shall we sit down for a minute?

(they sit)

The Enclosure! Don't you think it likely to be excessively hot?

Mrs. Verulam

Why especially hot in the Enclosure?

Rodney

Well, you know, it is so much more crowded than any other part of the course. Don't you think so?

Mrs. Verulam

Where else shall I go?

Rodney

I have ventured to take a couple of excellent boxes. You see one or two of our party—Mr. Ingerstall and Mr. Bush have not got cards for the Enclosure.

Mrs. Verulam

It is very good and thoughtful of you. Still, I think I shall go to the Enclosure. Mr. Van Adam is anxious to see what it is like.

Rodney (stiffening)

Indeed.

Mrs. Verulam

And then, there are all my friends, especially Lady Sage and—

Rodney

Lady Sage grows a little wearisome, I fancy.

Mrs. Verulam

Do you think so? Oh, I love her recollections.

Rodney

I think her too historical for hot summer weather, I confess—and then, her insatiable appetite for dates.

Mrs. Verulam

Oh, surely she wouldn't eat dates in the Enclosure.

Rodney

The dates of battles, dear lady, not dried fruits. Really, if you prefer to go to the Enclosure, I strongly, very strongly advise you to avoid Lady Sage. She is agreeable in a drawing room, but very Crimean, I do assure you, on a race-course. Do give me your word. I cannot bear to see you bored!

Mrs. Verulam

You are all kindness. I must go to the Enclosure. But I shall probably not see Lady Sage.

Rodney (aside)

Thank God!

(Reenter the Duke with Bush and several others.)

Mrs. Verulam

Oh, Mr. Bush.

Bush

You've got nice company here!

Mrs. Verulam

What?

Bush

Well, I'm blowed! You've got nice company.

Mrs. Verulam'

I hope so, indeed.

Bush

Mad, I suppose. Mad as Moses!

Mrs. Verulam

Ah, Mr. Bush, you mustn't make joke of so serious a subject as madness.

Bush

Joke! There's no joke! Where's the joke of being potted at like a rook in January? Joke, indeed—joke!

Mrs. Verulam

A rook in January?

Bush

Ah, if I'd have stayed, he'd have had me. I wasn't eight paces off him.

Duke

Unless the man's a remarkably poor shot, I must say, I think Mr. Bush stood in some slight danger. Did you not stay then?

Bush

Stay? Not I! I just ducked down on all fours and came back like a beast through the rhododendrons.

Duke (pleasantly)

A very sensible posture and mode of exit under the circumstances. (to Mrs. Verulam) Who's your sportsman?

Mrs. Verulam

I have no idea. Oh, Mr. Bush, I can scarcely tell you how grieved I am, how horrified I am, that you should have been so nearly murdered—and so soon after your arrival, too.

Bush

I should think so! A nice thing to happen to a respectable man!

Mrs. Verulam (bitterly)

Mr. Rodney, you never told me there was a murderer living in this neighborhood!

Rodney

I never knew it.

(to Bush)

Where did this incident occur?

Bush

I was walking in the garden looking at the mistakes the gardener here's been making.

Rodney

Yes, yes?

Bush

Presently, I came to a bit of a pond, with flowers afloating on it.

Rodney

Ah—and a cottage on the farther side?

Bush

Ay, where he fires from.

Rodney

The Bun Emperor.

Duke

Very unsportsmanlike to shoot from cover. Game haven't got a chance.

Bush

You're right there, chum, they haven't. Not unless they're as quick at dropping on all fours as I am.

Rodney

But, did you do anything?

Bush

No. I saw a fattish, smallish feller and a fattish, smallish woman by his side, staring out.

Rodney

The Empress, too. Well?

Bush

I didn't take any great account of them at first. I put my stick across the water to lay hold of some of the lilies, when, what does the fattish man do, but shout out: "If you do it, I'll skin you"— I didn't choose to notice his nonsense, and I just got hold of a lily when what do I see, but him with a gun at his shoulder about to fire away. So away I came, like a beast through the bush.

Rodney

The Bun Emperor is very touchy about his property.

Duke

A defender of the rights of property. A good conservative.

Mrs. Verulam

Still, he goes too far. Mr. Rodney, I must ask you to be kind enough to tell the Bun Emperor that I cannot have my house party shot at. Make it perfectly clear, please. As a hostess, I cannot, and will not, permit anything of that kind.

Rodney

Certainly, certainly. I see your point of view.

BLACKOUT

ACT II
SCENE 3

When the lights go up, Rodney is explaining the situation with the Bun Emperor to Mr. Bush and Mrs. Verulam.

Rodney (to Bush)

You are perfectly safe; you will not be hurt, I can promise you. Nobody will attempt to injure you.

Mrs. Verulam

You have persuaded him then? I knew you would have weight with him.

Rodney

My dear lady, I am happy to say that you have been totally misinformed as to the circumstances.

Bush (growling)

What? What?

Rodney (standing his ground)

Totally and absolutely misinformed.

Mrs. Verulam

Really, Mr. Rodney, what are you saying? Mr. Bush has been shot at.

Rodney (blandly)

I beg your pardon. I beg your pardon.

Bush

If I hadn't dropped, I shouldn't be here now.

Rodney

I assure you, my dear Mr. Bush, that you are laboring under an entire delusion. You might, with perfect safety, have retained an upright posture. It's true that Mr. Lite made use of some hasty, inconsiderate words about skinning—

Bush (triumphantly)

There!

(roaring)

What did I say?

Rodney (aside)

Of which I entirely approve.

(aloud)

But, the words were rather metaphysical. As to the firing, however, you are quite mistaken. What you took for a gun was merely a large telescope. When you thought you were being shot at, you were merely being looked at.

Bush (indignant, he knows what he knows)

Telescope, indeed! Telescope, I dare say.

Rodney (smugly)

There is an appreciable difference between the two operations. I think you will allow that. So, you see, Mr. Lite can hardly be blamed at all.

Mrs. Verulam

He should be more careful the way he looks at people!

Duke

Well, well, it's good it's all settled. It's going to be a long day at Ascot tomorrow, and a top hat is not very comfortable in the heat.

Bush

Top hats are rubbish. I've only brought a straw.

Rodney (flabbergasted)

But—

Bush

I shan't wear naught but a straw tomorrow.

Duke

I hate to be overdressed.

Rodney

I beg your pardon.

(trembling)

I beg your pardon, but I must venture to say that I feel certain Major Clement will turn a straw hat off the lawn.

Mrs. Verulam

I quite agree with Mr. Bush, a straw hat is much more sensible.

Rodney (in anguish)

Merciful heavens—

Mrs. Verulam

But, sometimes custom must be adhered to. Don't you think so, Mr. Bush?

Bush (surprised)

Eh?

Mrs. Verulam (reasonably)

Every man will be wearing a top hat tomorrow.

Bush

I've hoed and I've planted in a straw hat for thirty years.

Rodney (quickly)

There's no hoeing and planting on a race-course.

Duke

It would make the going a bit heavy.

Mrs. Verulam

I fancy, Mr. Bush, that as you will not have an opportunity of hoeing tomorrow, you will find it really pleasanter to be as everyone else is.

Bush

I haven't a-brought one. I say, I've only brought a straw.

Rodney

We must send a man to Windsor.

(to Harrison who is passing by)

Kindly bring us a yard measure.

Harrison

Oh, sir, oh, on no account.

CURTAIN

ACT III
SCENE 4

Same as in Act II. It is late the next night.

Mrs. Verulam

Where is Mr. Bush and Mr. Ingerstall?

Rodney (lazily)

I can't imagine.

Duchess

I dare say Mr. Bush is on a roundabout (merry-go-round). You say he is fond of being rustic, Mrs. Verulam?

Mrs. Verulam

Yes, but not in that way, I hope.

Duchess

It all goes together, love for the country and a passion for riding wooden horses to the sound of music. Depend upon it, Mr. Bush is on a roundabout.

Mrs. Verulam

Dear me! Mr. Rodney—

Rodney

If Mr. Bush is fond of horse exercise, I think he should be permitted to enjoy it in all freedom.

Duke

There's a great deal of knack in sitting a wooden horse. Some people never acquire it. I knew a very excellent clergyman who was thrown three times by a deal cob which his cook rode perfectly the very first try. Miss Bindler, You ought always to give a horse of that material its head. If you try to hold him, you're done.

Pearl

Do you like Ascot, Mr. Van Adam?

Van Adam

It's heavenly. Like a dream.

Pearl

Have you nothing of the kind in America?

Van Adam

How can we when we have no aristocracy? Oh, I should like to make it my life's mission to create a grand aristocracy. I would begin by getting baronets—they should be the thin edge of the wedge—and everything else would follow.

Duke

To Burke: instead of battle, an army of armorial bearings!

Duchess (to Mrs. Verulam)

Is Mr. Van Adam to be much longer with you?

Mrs. Verulam

I am afraid not in London. But we may go to Paris together in a week or two.

Duchess

Indeed!

(furiously)

Indeed!

Mrs. Verulam (coolly)

Or on the continent.

Rodney (to himself)

Is she mad?

(Enter Mr. Bush and Mr. Ingerstall. Bush's top hat is askew, and he has coconuts under his arm.)

Ingerstall

I would give one year of my life to take Mr. Bush to Montmartre. How he would appreciate it. He understands the exquisite poetry of vulgarity. He knows the bizarre effect of the roundabout—he—

Duchess

The roundabout? Didn't I say so?

Duke

You've been riding? Good exercise. Did you get a decent horse?

Bush

Haw!

Ingerstall

Splendid animal. I rode a pink, he a delicate green. I really never enjoyed Ascot so much—never!

Mrs. Verulam (delighted)

How original you are, and how bravely simple.

Rodney (aside)

She is mad!

Mrs. Verulam

Should we not all learn to find pleasure in what nature provides us? Instead of creating artificial amusements to titillate our baser appetites?

Van Adam (musing)

Does nature provide apple green horses?

Rodney (quivering with indignation)

Nature? Nature is scarcely decent!

Duke

And all the better for that!

Mrs. Verulam

The true path of pleasure lies where we never seek it, far, far from the conventions with which we surround ourselves. Oh, why, why are we so blind?

Rodney

I beg your pardon, I can see perfectly well—and—

Mrs. Verulam

You think you can see—as the blind man does when he mistakes men for trees walking.

Rodney

I never made any such mistake. I never in my life supposed that I saw a tree taking active exercise. Really, I must protest.

Mrs. Verulam

Your very protestations prove your sad condition. But I, at least, will be blind no longer. Mr. Bush has opened my eyes. Mr. Bush stands to me for virtue.

Duchess

And what does Mr. Van Adam stand for?

Mrs. Verulam (sweetly, slyly)

Oh, everything.

(to the Duchess)

Mr. Bush, you must know, is full of maxims.

Duchess

Dear me! Is he related to a copy book?

Mrs. Verulam

Oh no! Not maxims of that kind. His are founded upon observation of the world, of the earth. Aren't they, Mr. Bush?

Bush

There's naught like pea-poddin.

Mrs. Verulam (wonderingly)

Yes—yes.

Bush

Look after the sheep and the sheep'll look after you.

Duchess

I don't know that I should care to be looked after by a sheep. I don't consider a sheep to be an efficient animal.

Bush

They wont a deal of mendin, a deal of mendin.

Duke (yawning)

Because they have no minds!

Mrs. Verulam

It's what we bring to a thing, isn't it?

Duchess

What would you bring to a sheep?

Bush

Swedes to a sheep. Swedes. The stick to a woman.

Duke (delighted)

You believe in the rights of man, Mr. Bush? Eh? Eh? You stick to the old dispensation—the walnut tree cure? What? What?

Pearl

I should be very sorry for the man who laid a finger on me. Very!

Mrs. Verulam

Oh, Mr. Bush is only joking.

Duchess (staring straight at Mrs. Verulam)

A great many women would be the better for a whipping these days.

Bush

Never give a bullock sulfur, never do it, or you'll repent of it.

Duke

And how about the bullock?

Bush

Let the bullock alone, and the bullock'll let you alone.

(Bush falls asleep, or appears to.)

Rodney (aside)

The Lord is my Shepherd—

Ingerstall

He's asleep, isn't he?

Duchess (startled)

Asleep? Who?

Ingerstall (pulling out a sketchbook and rapidly sketching the sleeping giant)

Yes, he is. I've got something to show you.

Mrs. Verulam (hastily tugging up her skirts)

What is it? Is it alive?

Ingerstall

I fancy it is. Look at that!

Duchess

It's very like. Very true to life. Don't you think so, Mrs. Verulam?

Mrs. Verulam (looking)

Is it a bullock?

Ingerstall (pained)

A bullock! It's Bush!

Bush (startled)

Bush! Who's a-wanting me? Is it time to begin hoeing?

(silence)

Who wants Bush, eh?

Ingerstall

I do. I ask you: is that a bullock, or is it you? Come, come, I ask you? Is that a bullock, or is it you?

Bush

Me! Me! What d'yer want?

Ingerstall

What I say! What I say!

Bush (getting up and bending over Ingerstall's chair, holding both its arms in his gigantic paws)

This, me!

Duke (egging him on)

Go it!

Bush (bellowing at Ingerstall)

I ask you, is this here a bullock, or is it me?

Ingerstall (frightened, after a pause)

It's a bullock.

Bush (looking around triumphantly)

That's all right.

(Mrs. Verulam and Mr. Van Adam exchange a smile.)

Duchess (aside, intercepting the glance)

They're using Pearl.

(getting up)

Good night!

(exit)

Bush

The Duchess is very quick on her pins. Did she enter a walking race?

Duke

Not since I married her.

Bush

She should. She'd stand a ten to one chance.

(Bush falls back to sleep. After a bit of mimed conversation, the others go out. The light dims, then an old-fashioned telephone bell rings, repeatedly and wakes Bush.)

Emperor's Voice

Are you there? Damn you! Are you or aren't you there? Damn you! Are you there? Did I or did I not tell you you was to watch all night and be at the tube at three o'clock? Did I tell you or didn't I? If you aren't at the tube in another five minutes, tomorrow you shall be turned into the streets as surely as you are a living man! Into the streets you shall go, bag and baggage! Do you hear?

(Bush, waking up, lights a candle and looks around. He finally finds the telephone, but has obviously never seen a telephone before. More furious ringing!)

Emperor's Voice

Are you there? Where are you? Where the blazes are you? Damn you, are you or aren't you there? What do you mean by it? Did I or did I not tell you to be there at three o'clock? Did I or did I not?

Bush

No!

Emperor

Oh, you're there at last, are you? I wonder you have the impudence to come. Keep me dancing here for an hour and more!

Bush

Keep on dancing! Keep it up!

Emperor

What do you say?

Bush

Dance away and be damned!

Emperor

Tomorrow I'll skin you! D'ye hear what I say? Tomorrow when you come round with your report, I'll skin you!

Bush

I shan't come round.

Emperor

(cannot believe his ears)

What?

Bush

Go to blazes!

Emperor

Why, damn you—

Bush

Keep your hair on!

Emperor

You, you—

Bush

There's naught like pea-poddin.

Emperor

I'll, I'll—

Bush

Look after the sheep and the sheep'll look after you.

Emperor

Damn, damn. Double damn!

Bush

Never give a bullock sulfur, or you'll repent of it. Keep on dancing. Go to blazes, go! How's yourself? Has the dancing done for yer? Would you like to skin me now? Come on, I'm waiting to be skinned. Yes, I am. I'm ready for it. Come and skin me, come!

(Bush, greatly satisfied with himself, laughs and goes out. After a minute a sleepy Harrison comes in. The telephone bells rings again.)

Emperor

If you don't come round, as sure as you're a living man, at the end of the week, I'll tear you limb from limb.

Harrison (frightened)

Sir!

Emperor

If you don't come round—I say—by eight—

Harrison

But, sir, I shall be round. Depend upon me; I shall be there to the moment. Oh, most decidedly.

Emperor

Oh, you're coming, are you?

Harrison

Oh, most certainly, sir. Could you doubt it?

Emperor

Then, as soon as you come, I'll skin you!

Harrison

Sir!

Emperor

At eight, I'll skin you to the moment, I will; and Mrs. Lite says exactly similar.

(Harrison faints.)

BLACKOUT

ACT III
SCENE 5

The Bun Emperor's cottage the next morning. Harrison approaches a little bridge leading to the cottage. The Emperor spots him and comes out ready to do battle.

Emperor

Come on!

Harrison (not budging an inch)

Sir!

Emperor

Come on, or you'll repent of it to the last hour of your mortal life, you will.

Harrison

Oh, by all means, most certainly. Oh, most decidedly yes. Oh, indeed—rely on—

Emperor

Make haste!

Empress

Oh, you wicked, ungrateful man!

Emperor

Come in, this moment!

(Harrison does not move)

Come in! Do you defy me?

Empress

Wicked, wicked man!

Harrison

Let me explain, sir. Oh, indeed, I will explain.

Emperor

Coward! You know I can't come out to get at you! You know I've given my word to that fiddle-faced feller! Coward.

Empress

Cowardly custard!

Harrison

I will not come in to be skinned. No, I will not! No, I will not, if I stay here till the Doomsday, no, indeed!

(The Empress and Emperor hold a whispered imperial conference.)

Emperor (furiously)

You'd better come in.

(Harrison does not move, and this precipitates another whispered conference.)

Emperor

I'll keep my hands from you, but come in you shall!

Harrison

Sir!

Emperor

Come in, I say, and I'll keep my hands off you.

Harrison

And the missus, sir? She will not attempt to injure me? Oh, dear, no, no, on no account whatever.

Empress (grudgingly)

I won't either.

Narrator [who makes his first and last appearance here]

Mr. Harrison's fear was extreme, so extreme that his mind became brilliant, and he formed a plan of campaign.

Harrison

Lord, sir, Lord. The doings of the Londoners. Their goings on!

Their manners with the telephone! Their tamperings with the parrots. Their proceedings of a nighttime. Lord, sir, Lord! I am driven mad. It is no wonder, oh no, indeed! By no means. On no account whatever!

Emperor

The worst has come, Henrietta, the worst has come along.

Harrison

And worse than that, sir, you may depend upon me.

Empress

Our little home. They are breaking up our home. What did I say? What did I always and ever say?

(The Emperor and Empress weep.)

Harrison

It began yesterday. It began with them throwing me from one of your hammocks in which I was concealed to watch, according to your orders. Throwing me out on my face, sir, flat—and laughing at what they had done.

Empress

The brutes! The inhuman things! The brutes!

Harrison

It was Mr. Rodney what done it with his own hands—and Mrs. Verulam standing by and laughing to split her sides.

Empress

Hussy! Thieving hussy!

Harrison

But there was worse to come. I was watching Mr. Bush according to your directions at the telephone, punctual to the moment—when her ladyship came down dressed only in a shawl—and then Mr. Bush took me from behind, sir, like a coward, and if I escaped with my life, it is a wonder. Oh most decidedly, a wonder!

Empress

And only in her shawl!

Emperor

My dear, my love, remember the presence of Mr. Harrison.

Empress (low to the Emperor)

I'll skin you when he's gone!

Emperor

Mr. Harrison, I was mistook. You have done your duty, and myself and Mrs. Lite shall not forget it. You will receive those perquisites which are your bounden due. Though, whatever you meant through the telephone, mercy only knows.

Empress

Yes, mercy knows.

Harrison

Through the telephone, sir. I was mad, sir. They had drove me mad—most decidedly, yes they had.

Emperor

Was you mad when you says dance away and be damned?

Harrison

Sir?

Emperor

Was you mad when you says to Mrs. Lite— Go to blazes—?

Harrison

Oh, most decidedly, oh undoubtedly I was, sir.

Emperor

And when you tells me to give a bullock sulfur?

Harrison

Did I, sir?

Emperor

Mr. Harrison, you did. And I was to keep my hair on, look after the sheep, and again be damned, Mr. Harrison.

Harrison

It was madness, sir. It was indeed. It must have been, oh, not a doubt of it! There can be no question of a bullock—sulfur—dance and be damned. Oh dear! Oh dear! It was madness, oh most certainly.

Emperor

Enough, Mr. Harrison, enough! Mrs. Lite and me, believing that you was driven mad, will overlook the expressions which should not have come from you to such as us. Enough, Mr. Harrison, enough.

BLACKOUT

ACT III
SCENE 6

Ribton Marches, later that afternoon. The Duke, the Duchess, Lady Pearl, and Mr. Bush are in the gardens.

Duchess

Dear me, what an influx of gardeners. It gives the grounds a crowded appearance. This must be a terribly expensive place to keep up.

Bush

If they keep on as they're keepin' now, there won't be a bloomin' flower within fifty miles of this place tomorrow.

Duke

If those men were my gardeners, I should have them up before the nearest magistrate for damaging my property.

(to a waiter who offers tea)

No tea, thanks. A whisky.

Pearl

How self-conscious they look!

Duchess

Gardeners always do. They think themselves the only artistic people among the wage earning classes. Silly!

(Enter Mr. Rodney, dripping wet.)

Duke

Wet? Much better to take your liquids internally.

Rodney

Wet? I am saturated! I am drenched! These liberties are really unpardonable. I must change.

(exit)

Duchess

How very strange. They all appear to be watching us. Are they a party of mesmerists, do you think? Really, it can scarcely be mere idle curiosity.

Pearl

That one chap looks to me like a third-rate detective.

Duke

They all look like third-rate detectives.

Van Adam (shocked)

Detectives!

(aside, glancing around warily)

Do they know?

Duke (aside)

Must be after me, again. Been shadowed for forty-five years.

(drawing Bush aside)

See those men?

Bush

What?

Duke

See those men who watered Rodney?

Bush

Ha, ha. Rodney'll be sprouting. Rodney'll be sprouting.

Duke

They are detectives.

Bush

What are they a-doing? What are they here for?

Duke

I'll let you into a secret. They're here for me. You're a bit of a dog yourself. You want watching, too, what? The husband who would trust you would soon find himself in Queer Street—what?

(goes off, laughing)

Bush (aside)

Here's a go. The Duke must have set them on me. The Duchess must be mad for me. Here's a bit of fun. I'll have me a lie-down.

(Bush sits and falls asleep. Reenter Rodney in a dry suit.)

Pearl

I hope you are none the worse for your immersion?

Rodney

I fear I cannot hope to escape rheumatic fever. To do so would indeed be foolish optimism.

Duke

It's not every man who can say, with truth, he's been followed by detectives almost five and forty years.

Van Adam

It is not every man who can say anything at all with truth.

Duke

Do you doubt my word?

Van Adam

I'll believe yours, if you'll believe mine.

Duke

What? Then, you're followed by detectives, too?

(Lady Pearl comes up to Van Adam and the Duke.)

Pearl

Do you think it right to be happy, Mr. Van Adam? Do you think we are meant to have any joy here?

Van Adam

Oh, dear, no. No, no! When we think all is going well, we are sure to see the gardeners. The gardeners are certain to come upon us.

Pearl

Do you think the misery of the world is caused by gardeners?

Van Adam

I do, indeed. I am perfectly certain of it.

Pearl

How strange! Why is it?

Van Adam

Because—we are all gardeners. Do we not garden each other's

souls?

Pearl

How exquisitely thoughtful you are!

Duchess

Well, Mr. Bush, how do you like the great world?

Bush (waking)

Eh?

(glancing suspiciously at the Duke)

Eh?

Duchess

Do you find it very different from your marshes? I suppose there are only frogs there?

Bush

When I catch a frog, I go for it.

Duchess

When? And where does the frog go?

Bush

Not far, not far!

Duchess

Dear me! I am afraid you're a bloodthirsty person like most men. But you're all the same; you must kill something. One man stalks a deer, another a frog. You shoot, I suppose?

Bush

No, I don't. Frog shootin' wouldn't pay. They go too slow.

Duchess

Heavens! The gardeners are all waiting at table. That creature with the sauce boat was clipping the hedge and—

Bush

Hush, give over!

Duchess

Why? They—

Bush

Give over, I tell yer!

Duchess

What is it?

Bush

They ain't gardeners.

Duchess

What! They are really footmen?

Bush

They ain't footmen!

Duchess

Not footmen! Then, what sort of servants are they?

Bush

They ain't servants. Give over. Don't talk so loud.

Duchess

Not servants! Then what are they here for?

Bush

They're here for us.

Duchess

For us?

Bush

You and me—me and you!

Duchess

Me and you!

Bush

Ay, it's a go, ain't it?

Duchess

But, what on earth are they? Not, no—not dentists?

Bush

They're coppers! Don't holler!

Duchess

Coppers!?

Bush

Police. Private dicks.

Duchess

Private dicks?

Bush

A-watching of you and me. Detectives! Give over, now; here's one a-coming.

(The detective servant hands some tea clumsily.)

Duchess

But, who put them to watch us?

Bush

It's his doing.

Duchess

The Duke?

Bush

He thinks you and me is a-going on together.

(The Duchess faints.)

CURTAIN

ACT IV
SCENE 7

Same as last scene in Act III. The next evening. The Duke accosts Mr. Bliggins, head of the gardeners/detectives.

Duke (affably)

What's your name?

Bliggins

Bliggins, sir.

Duke

Very well, Bliggins. Can you keep a quiet tongue in your head?

Bliggins

I can be dumb, sir, when necessary.

Duke

How nice to command your infirmities at will. You don't go blind when you go dumb, what?

Bliggins

I can prevent it, sir, if I am induced.

Duke

Do you know which of the gentlemen is Mr. James Bush?

Bliggins

Ain't he the thin gent as Smithers set to and soaked?

Duke

Hmm?

Bliggins

Beg pardon, sir?

Duke

Can you serve two masters, Mr. Bliggins?

Bliggins

I can, sir, if I am induced—paid in a proper manner, as you might say.

Duke

Very well. First, let me say, I know you. You're a detective, and you've been put here to watch me. Be quiet, man!

(hushing Bliggins' protests)

I ought to know a third-rate detective by this time, considering that for five and forty years—but, that is no matter. Lord Arthur Kempton's your employer, no doubt, or Sir John Morton. Hold your tongue! I've no time to hear your lies. Watch me as much as you like—but keep an eye on the man with the red beard.

Bliggins

Him as was talking so loud with the Duchess when she fainted.

Duke

The very man. James Bush: watch him!

Bliggins

I will, sir.

Duke

Day and night.

Bliggins

The charge for night duty—(the Duke presses money into his hands) I will, sir—day and night.

Duke

Now go away, and get dumb.

(Exit the Duke and Mr. Bliggins in different directions. After a moment, enter the Duchess, Mrs. Verulam, and Mr. Van Adam.)

Duchess

I have known you for a long time, Mrs. Verulam. I remember you as a toddler.

Mrs. Verulam

Thank you.

Duchess

Not everyone can say as much.

Mrs. Verulam

I dare say not. No.

Duchess

Those were innocent days.

Mrs. Verulam

Toddlers are generally innocent, I suppose.

Duke

Innocent and open-hearted.

Mrs. Verulam

Yes.

Duchess

In after life, it is different. The respectability of childhood becomes impaired.

Mrs. Verulam (innocently)

Does it?

Duchess (staring pointedly at Mrs. Verulam and Mr. Van Adam)

Does it not?

Mrs. Verulam

I don't know.

Duchess

I should have thought you did.

Mrs. Verulam

Why?

Duchess

Let me give you a piece of advice.

Mrs. Verulam

Oh, I like advice.

Duchess

Get rid of Mr. Van Adam. I speak as a true friend.

Mrs. Verulam

Why should I get rid of him?

Duchess (turning purple)

There are many reasons.

Mrs. Verulam

I know of none. Poor boy. He needs me in his loneliness.

Duchess

Good gracious! Gracious heavens!

Mrs. Verulam

We ought to be kind to those whom the world has treated cruelly. Poor Mr. Van Adam. Poor, dear fellow.

(sighing)

Duchess

I am very ill. I am much upset.

(The Duchess exits. As she leaves, the Duke peeps in; he is watching for any sign or signal between the Duchess and Mr. Bush. Van Adam approaches Mrs. Verulam, and Mr. Rodney darts in to prevent any possibility of a tête-à-tête.)

Van Adam

I do so want to tell you something. Have you read the World?

Mrs. Verulam

No; but I have something to— Oh! Good night, Mr. Rodney; I hope your rheumatic fever will be better in the morning.

Rodney

You are very good to say so, but I am thoroughly prepared for the worst.

(Rodney obstinately stays put. Van Adam clenches her fists. Bush ambles up to say good night.)

Mrs. Verulam

Good night, Mr. Bush. I must tell you what an impression your conduct at dinner made upon me.

Bush

Go along with yer! Rubbish! She's a deal too old.

(Bush goes out and sits with the Duke who has been peeping in.)

Mrs. Verulam (puzzled)

Now, what did he mean by that?

Ingerstall

Damn it, there's no absinthe. In Paris, one is not deprived of necessities as one is in England. Why don't I live in Paris?

(to Bliggins)

Where the devil's the absinthe?

Bliggins

Beg pardon, sir.

(Bliggins indicates to the Duke that he has been watching Bush.)

Ingerstall

Ventrebleu! Where is the absinthe, man? Haven't I told you that I don't drink those Scotch and Irish abominations?

Bliggins

Certainly not, sir, certainly not.

Ingerstall (recognizing Bliggins)

It's a gardener.

Duke (overhearing)

A gardener, Ingerstall! What nonsense!

Ingerstall (stubbornly)

It is. I observed him this afternoon. I remember his nose like a teapot, his eyes like marbles, his retreating chin, and protruding forehead, perfectly. His arms are too long for his body, and his legs too short for his height. He would make an admirable cartoon, admirable. I remember thinking so.

Bliggins (weeping)

Oh, sir.

(Exit Bliggins in tears.)

Ingerstall (calling after him)

You're a beautiful subject, beautiful.

Duke (viciously)

You've frightened the fellow. Why didn't you leave him alone?

Ingerstall

Leave a monstrosity alone! Leave a human grotesque in ignorance of his superb infirmity! I'll draw him this minute.

(Exit Ingerstall in great determination.)

Mrs. Verulam

Would you mind fetching my fan, Mr. Rodney? I believe I left it on the table in the magenta boudoir.

Rodney (determined not to leave)

Forgive me if I send a servant for it. I can scarcely walk; this fever seems increasing upon me.

Mrs. Verulam

Dear, dear. Then you must not dream of going to the races.

Rodney

The fresh air will do me good.

Mrs. Verulam

Mr. Van Adam can escort me. You must be wrapped at once in cotton wool and put in a darkened room with the temperature at least eighty.

Rodney (fiercely)

I consider it my duty not to spoil your week by—by giving way (looking at Van Adam) to illness, perhaps even to death.

Mrs. Verulam

Mr. Rodney! I have been thinking a cooling draught would do you good.

Rodney (hysterically)

It is most good of you, but I am perfectly cool—perfectly cool. Nothing is more dangerous to a rheumatic than a thorough draught.

Pearl

It would be fatal, simply fatal. It would carry him off in the twinkling of an eye.

Van Adam (aside)

If only something would.

Mrs. Verulam

I meant a drink, not a breeze. Marriner could mix it for you, Mr. Rodney.

Rodney (wildly)

You are too kind, but I never take medicine. I prefer to put my trust in Providence and hope for the best.

Mrs. Verulam

I think that even the bishops and clergy would say that we Christians ought to assist the operation of Providence—with appropriate medicine.

Van Adam (aside)

Castor oil, for my money.

Mrs. Verulam

Mr. Rodney, your fever makes you act very strangely.

(she leaves for a moment)

Rodney

Yes, I suppose it does. You are not going to retire so early, Mr. Van Adam?

Van Adam

I am dead beat.

Rodney (clutching at Van Adam)

Then a smoke will do you good! You must have a cigar, you must! A drink, my dear Van Adam—a long drink, a strong drink.

Duke

Hullo! Van Adam, sitting up! Bravo!

Van Adam (shrugging helplessly to Mrs. Verulam)

Well—

Duke

Have a light?

(giving a cigar, which Van Adam holds diffidently)

Won't it draw?

Van Adam

No, I don't think it will. I'll—I think I'll have a cigarette, thanks.

Bush

A pipe's the thing—a pipe and a fistful of Bristol Bird's Eye.

Van Adam

Oh no, not a pipe.

Duke

Come and sit here. Now the women are gone, we can say what we like, what?

Van Adam

Yes, we can, I suppose.

Rodney

A very good cigar, this.

Duke

I dare say it is—when it's lighted.

(Rodney goes red from embarrassment, then lights eight to ten matches at the same time.)

Duke

Well done, Rodney! Set the place on fire! Tell us a good story, Rodney, one of your rorty ones.

Rodney (shriveling)

I fear—I fear I am scarcely in the rorty vein tonight. Tomorrow, the next day, perhaps.

Duke

Well, then, you tip us one, Van Adam. Go ahead.

Van Adam

Some girls in Florida do such lovely needlework.

Duke

Lovely needlework! That's a funny beginning for a pink 'un. Well?

Van Adam

They sit all day in the sun—

Duke

Damned silly girls! Spoil their complexions. They should go into the shade, what? What? What?

Ingerstall (peeping in abruptly)

I knew a grisette once who lived on the fourth floor in the Rue des Martyres.

(Ingerstall disappears suddenly when all stare at him.)

Van Adam (clearing throat)

They sit in the sun and work for their living.

Duke

Deuced tiresome, what Rodney?

Rodney

I confess I should prefer to be under the trees.

Duke

Well, go on, Van Adam, go on.

Van Adam

Well—er, well—that's all.

Duke

All! Oh, come, I say, hang it, you're pulling our legs!

Van Adam

Oh, no. Why should I do such a thing?

Duke

But, hang it, your story'd do for a school treat or a grandmother's meeting. That's not the sort of thing Rodney cares for, what, Rodney?

(digging Rodney in the ribs and causing him to knock over a vase)

Smashing up the furniture now, after trying to set the whole place on fire?

Rodney

An accident! Merely an unlikely accident, Duke. I shall make it good to Mr. Lite.

Duke

If you don't, he'll probably skin you.

Rodney

Oh, really, really, I should not submit for a moment to an indignity of that nature.

Duke

Well, I dare say, even a moment of being flayed would inconvenience a chap. But, come, give us a limerick.

Rodney

I don't know any. I've never been to Ireland.

Duke (puzzled)

Ireland? What's Ireland got to do with it?

Rodney (innocently)

Everything, I should suppose.

Duke (disputing)

Anyone would think we were a lot of damned old women. We might as well be Sunday school teachers at a Methodist funeral.

(Bush snores loudly.)

Rodney (frightened)

What's that?

Duke (sneeringly)

Oh—it's only Mr. Bush, asleep!

Rodney

He sleeps very loud for decent society.

Duke

He does sleep very loud.

(whispering to Rodney)

Does anything occur to you, Rodney?

Rodney

I beg pardon.

(Van Adam takes the chance and exits.)

Duke

Does anything occur to you with regard to this damned uproarious sleep?

Rodney

No, nothing at all. What should occur to me?

Duke (contemptuously)

Oh, Lord, I don't know. I don't know.

Rodney (realizing Van Adam has eluded him)

Why, where the deuce is Van Adam? He's gone—he's— Does anything occur to you, Duke?

Duke

What?

Rodney

I say, does anything occur to you, Duke?

Duke

What about?

Rodney

About Van Adam's sudden going off in this strange manner?

Duke

No, except he's like some damned old woman. Americans are such puritans. What should occur?

Rodney

Oh, dear—nothing, nothing at all. I—I—Good night.

(Exit Rodney, hurriedly in some confusion.)

Duke

Well, of all the sniveling, psalm singing, non-conformist Salvation Army sets of fellows that ever I met in my life—this one takes the—

(Bush snores)

That fellow's as broad awake as I am—and broader! But, I'll be even with him, crafty as he is!

(poking Bush in the ribs)

Nice and quiet here.

(Bush starts)

I say, nice and quiet here. Nobody about.

Bush (waking)

What if there isn't?

Duke

I beg your pardon?

Bush

I say, what if there isn't anybody about?

Duke

Oh, nothing, nothing! I was only thinking what games might be carried on in a big house like this and nobody the wiser.

Bush

Was you?

Duke

Midnight revels, what? What? What?

(digging him in the ribs)

You're a dog!

Bush

Give over! I ain't a dog!

Duke

Yes, you are. I know you. I know all about it. Lady Drake's a fine woman—a damned fine woman!

Bush

Lady Drake, she's all right—go along with yer! She knows a thing or two. She's as downy as a goat in autumn, she is!

Duke

You like 'em downy, what? You like a crafty one? What?

Bush

Rather! Rather!

Duke

Because you're a downy one yourself? I know you!

Bush

Look after Lady Drake and she'll look after you.

Duke

And did you look after her in the hall at three o'clock, Mr. Bush? I saw you, I saw you both. I know all about it.

(aside)

I knew she was lying to me. I knew the fellow as a regular demon.

Bush (laying a big paw on the Duke's arm, confidentially)

She's a rascal.

Duke

Lady Drake?

Bush

She's a rascal! Set the gardeners on to her! She wants a-watching.

Duke

You're right. The gardeners should direct their attention to her. Shall I give them a hint to that effect?

Bush

Ay! Ay! Set them on to her! She wants a-watching!

Duke (aside)

Exquisite villain. Monument of evil.

(aloud)

I'll take your advice. I'll set them on to her.

(Bush relaxes and the Duke starts to leave, but runs into Bliggins.)

Duke

Watch that red-bearded rascal! Watch him! Never let him from under your eyes.

Bliggins

But, it's the black gent with the specs as is the dangerous one, sir.

Duke

This red-bearded villain—he's the man. He's the fiend, I tell you. Dog his footsteps. Creep after him. Run him down! You shan't repent of it. Hush, not a word!

(Bliggins conceals himself and starts to watch Bush who has dozed off again.)

Harrison's Voice

After setting fire to the 'ouse—oh, most decidedly, sir! Mr. Rodney is now smashing up furniture, Mrs. Lite, Chinese vases, sir. Oh, indeed, sir! And the Duke, ma'am, was splitting his sides with laughter while he done it. Oh, I'm keeping an eye on him.

(bumping into Bliggins who is crawling around)

Mrs. Bliggins, you were hired to watch, oh indeed!

Bliggins

I was watching, Mr. Harrison, sir. The red-bearded man—he's the fiend! Stalk him! I was doing it.

Harrison

Mr. Bliggins—them was no words of mine, oh, dear no, on no account whatever! My words to you was: watch the lot— Oh, most certainly.

(Bliggins and Mr. Harrison go out, the lights go very dark. Bush continues to snore. Then Van Adam and Mrs. Verulam steal in.)

Mrs. Verulam's Voice

Now—oh!

Van Adam

Shh! Be quiet, Daisy. It's only me. They're all asleep. Don't wake them.

Mrs. Verulam

I thought it was a ghost.

Van Adam

Can we sit down?

(sitting)

EEK! It's a cactus.

Mrs. Verulam

Over here. Now, I must tell you—

Van Adam

And, I must tell you—

Mrs. Verulam

Mrs. Rodney has heard from New York that your husband—

Van Adam

And I have heard from Sherlock Holmes, a detective I employ, that my husband—

Together

—Is in England.

Van Adam

—In Yorkshire. He may come to Ascot at any moment!

Mrs. Verulam

Do you want him back?

Van Adam

Back! What do you mean?

Mrs. Verulam

He wants you back. That's why he's come. He's discovered that you never—you know—

Van Adam

So. He's learned his lesson.

Mrs. Verulam

But you can't remarry him in trousers.

Van Adam

I shall take them off. At once.

Mrs. Verulam

But, if you do, what will happen to me?

Van Adam

To you?

Mrs. Verulam

My reputation will be restored. I shall be ruined.

Van Adam

Then I must disappear and take off my trousers.

Mrs. Verulam

And give up society?

Van Adam

I feel as you do, now. I don't care anymore. Love is the only thing. You were right.

Mrs. Verulam

Did I say that? Dear me!

Van Adam

You certainly did! What about Mr. Bush and Bungay Marsh?

Mrs. Verulam

Bungay—Bungay—your trousers.

Van Adam

Bungay my trousers! Surely, it would spoil them?

Mrs. Verulam

Listen. You want to change them, don't you? That's the place to do it. No one will look for us there. Let us go.

Van Adam

When?

Mrs. Verulam

Now!

Van Adam

In the middle of the night?

Mrs. Verulam

Yes.

Van Adam

How will we get there?

(Enter the Duchess above with a weak light.)

Duchess

Who dares to take off his trousers in this house?

Mrs. Verulam

Run!

(Exit Mrs. Verulam and Van Adam. The Duchess slips while coming down the stairs. Enter the Duke.)

Duke

I've caught you at last, have I?

Bush (waking)

What? What?

Duke (jumping over the Duchess to get at Bush)

You shall not escape me! Your blood—I'll have it!

Bush (running off quickly)

Catchin' comes before hangin'.

(The Duke follows Bush in hot pursuit. Enter Lady Pearl at the head of the stairs. She has a revolver.)

Pearl

This sort of thing won't do. It's time someone taught these robbers a lesson.

(firing her pistol six times)

Thieves! Thieves!

(Lady Pearl exits to reload. Enter Harrison.)

Harrison

If so much as the house is set afire, or the furniture is broke to pieces—

(Harrison bumps into the Duke, who is returning. The Duke attempts to strangle Harrison, but is beaten off and then goes to Rodney's door.)

Rodney's Voice

Don't dare to enter! I shall certainly kill the first man who enters.

Duke

Rodney, Rodney! Let me in, Rodney.

Rodney

If I sell my life, I shall sell it dearly. I will not be slain without a struggle.

Duke

Rodney, don't be a fool. Don't be an ass, Rodney.

Rodney

I will! Nothing shall prevent me, nothing on earth. I will, I will.

(The Duke finally enters and pulls Rodney out.)

Rodney

I will die here! I will not be killed in the open! I will die here.

Duke

Come out of it, Rodney. You must act for me in this affair.

Rodney

No, no. I will not come out.

Duke

Come out you shall.

Rodney (woebegone)

Do it mercifully, then. Why—It's you, Duke. I thought you were my friend.

(Lady Pearl, having reloaded her revolver, appears briefly on the stairs, firing again.)

Duke

Rodney, you're an ass. But, fool or ass, you must act for me in this affair. I've been trying to strangle that fellow Bush.

Rodney

Did you? Did you succeed in doing so, Duke?

Duke (bitterly)

He managed to get away from me. Just as I was on the point of choking the life out of him.

Rodney (with great feeling)

What a pity!

Duke (delighted)

Then, you will act for me?

Rodney

Yes, yes, with the greatest pleasure.

Duke (with good humor)

You're a man after all! We'll kill him yet, between us. This sort of business makes a man think.

Rodney

It does, it does, indeed!

Duke

Then it's settled! I shall search for the fellow first. If I find him here, I'll just finish him off. If not, he'll make a beeline for Bungay. We'll follow him there, force a duel on him and bury him in his own cabbage patch!

CURTAIN

ACT V
SCENE 8

Bungay Marshes. A small farm house with out buildings. Jacob Minnindick is hoeing.

Jacob

Darn it all. If it ain't 'im back already.

Bush

How's the vegs?

Jacob

Mortal spoilt by rain, darn 'em. What's brought you back so soon?

Bush

What's that t'yer? Why don't yer get to hoeing?

Jacob

Why don't ye get to them as drew ye from hoeing?

Bush

Shut yer head; I've done with 'em.

Jacob

Oh, I dessay. But, who's seen arter the mushrooms? Who's a-cared for them there mellins while ye was with 'em?

(A noise of horses off.)

Bush (hearing the noise)

What's that?

Jacob

'Osses.

Bush

Stand before me! Cover me up! Throw sprouts on me. Throw sprouts on me.

(Bush falls to the ground and tries to conceal himself. Enter the Duke and Rodney.)

Duke

You've pulled a hamstring in that horse, Rodney. Why the devil didn't you give him his head?

Rodney

Because I didn't dare, because I cannot—I—

Duke (seeing Jacob)

Here you, my man, can you tell me the way to the farm Bungay Marshes?

Jacob

Heh?

Duke

I want the farm, Bungay Marshes.

Jacob

What d'ye want 'un for?

Duke

What the deuce is that to you? Well, my man, don't you know where the farm is?

Jacob

Yes, I knows.

Duke

Where, then?

Jacob

'Ereabouts.

Duke

I know that.

Jacob

What did you arst me fer, then?

Bush (whispering)

Shovel the sprouts over me, d'ye hear? Cover me over!

Duke

I'll give you a taste of my whip if I have any more of your impudence. Tell me where the farm is, this moment.

Jacob

I have told ye.

Duke

Where is it?

Jacob

'Ereabouts.

Duke

Where the devil's hereabouts?

Jacob

Where yer standing!

Duke

Where I'm standing? Why didn't you say so?

Jacob

I did say so.

Duke

Where's your master? Is he back?

Jacob

Heh?

Duke

Where the deuce is your infernal master?

Jacob (coolly)

'Ereabouts.

Bush (whispering)

Cover me up, damn you.

Duke

Where the deuce is that?

Jacob

Where I'm standing.

Duke (seeing Bush)

You rascal—you infernal rascal! Then, I didn't strangle you after all?

Bush (rising)

Eh?

Duke

I didn't strangle you. But I will.

Rodney

Take a little time to think it over.

Duke

Rodney, hold your tongue. I thought I'd killed you.

Bush

You never touched me! I went too quick fer yer.

Duke

I strangled someone. Who could it have been?

Rodney

Perhaps a detective.

Duke

Bliggins, perhaps. Never mind. What does matter, is that I'm going to kill you. Do you hear, sir?

Bush

I ain't deaf.

Duke

Right here.

Rodney

I implore you to be calm. Don't make a scene. If you must kill him, do so quietly.

Duke

Choose your weapon.

Bush

Eh?

Duke

Choose your weapon. What do you generally fight with here?

Bush

Hoes. Allus fight with a hoe and never repented of it.

Duke

Hoes! Well, if you like—but I've never done so, I shall have to practice. That's only fair.

Rodney

Yes, yes. Take a week.

Duke

A week! An hour will be enough. Very well. Let it be hoes. Where can I get one?

Bush

At the Elephant and Drum.

Duke

Where the deuce is that?

Bush

The inn to Bungay. Down the road.

Duke

The very place, the very place. How far is it?

Bush

Half a mile.

Duke

I shall be back in an hour or two, then. Cheerio. Come, Rodney. If you try to get away, I'll follow you to the ends of the earth. This way, Rodney.

(Exit Duke purposefully and Rodney hesitantly. Bush and

Minnindick grunt at each other and resume hoeing. After a moment, the noise of a carriage.)

Bush

Whatever's that?

Jacob

A kerridge a-comin'.

Bush

What should a carriage come for?

(Noise of carriage stopping. Enter the Duchess.)

Duchess

Oh, Mr. Bush, Mr. Bush.

Bush

What's brought you a-here?

Duchess

Oh, Mr. Bush, you've ruined me! You have undone me, Mr. Bush.

Bush

Get along with yer!

Duchess

You have indeed! You must make reparation. You must go to the Duke, Mr. Bush. You must go to him and tell him how innocent I am.

Jacob

Innercent, does she say?

Duchess (clasping Bush's knees)

Oh, Mr. Bush! Do me justice. Set me right. Go to my husband and tell him what a true wife I have always been to him.

Bush

Give over! Give over now!

Duchess

I will not give over! I have followed you here, for you alone can tell the Duke there's nothing between—

(sound of carriage)

Oh, hide me! Hide me! There's a carriage coming! Oh, if I am seen here, I am lost forever.

Bush

Give over! Where can yer a-hide?

(The Duchess runs into the mushroom house.)

Jacob (protesting)

Not the mushroom house! She'll a-treadle down the spawn! She'll do a mischief on the mushrooms!

(Bush and Minnindick resume hoeing. Mrs. Verulam and Van Adam enter, arm in arm.)

Mrs. Verulam

How very peaceful it is! Here all is rest and happiness.

Van Adam

Quite so, dear.

Mrs. Verulam

It is like heaven.

Van Adam

By now everyone at Ribton Marches knows of our flight.

Mrs. Verulam (amused)

I wonder what the Duchess is saying.

Duchess's voice (from the mushroom house)

Oh, I shall be suffocated! The smell—of—of—

Van Adam

No doubt she is taking away your character.

Mrs. Verulam

I hate large, respectable women. Mr. Rodney will be terribly shocked at my running away like this.

Van Adam

Poor Mr. Rodney.

Mrs. Verulam

Why do you say poor? He's very rich.

Van Adam

Because— Oh, Daisy, you know quite well! At any rate, society will never have any more to do with a hostess who leaves a Duke and a Duchess stranded in the middle of Ascot week. You might get over murder more easily.

Mrs. Verulam

I suppose the Duke is furious.

Van Adam

It can't be helped if he is. There doesn't seem to be anybody about.

(Van Adam looks everywhere but at Bush and Minnindick, who continue hoeing.)

Mrs. Verulam

Let's go in. I can't wait to see you without your trousers.

Duchess

Little hussy!

Van Adam

I look ever so much better without them.

Duchess

Oh, I am going to faint at such talk. Ahh—the smell revived me.

Van Adam

Ah, ah, ah—

Mrs. Verulam

What is it?

Van Adam

There's someone coming down the road. Daisy, come, come! Two men are coming down the road.

(Mrs. Verulam and Van Adam go into the house.)

Jacob

They're gone into the house.

(A moment later Van Adam and Mrs. Verulam appear in an upper story window.)

Van Adam

It's my husband, I know it, I know it. What shall I do?

Mrs. Verulam

No! Good heavens! It's the Duke and Mr. Rodney carrying hoes.

Duke

I shall kill him without a doubt.

(The mushroom house door opens and shuts immediately.)

Rodney

Indeed, I fervently hope so. Still, we can never tell in these matters. You have made a will, I hope?

Duke

By Jove! Lucky you reminded me. Give me some paper.

Rodney

Paper?

Duke

Paper, so I can disinherit that false woman.

Duchess's voice

Ahh—I faint.

Rodney

Let me intercede.

Duke

Not a word.

Rodney

I don't have any paper.

Duke

Never mind. You will report my dying words, if it comes to that.

Rodney

Don't you think you'd better put it off a few hours? He's lying about in his garden.

(Bush continues to hoe.)

Duke

I intend to lay him out. Mr. Bush! Are you deaf, sir? Are you deaf and blind, sir?

Bush

Give over!

Duke

How dare you speak to me like that, sir? How dare you do it, sir? Do you suppose that because you have me out here in the country you can intimidate me, sir?

Bush

Get along with you!

Duke

I shall do nothing of the kind, sir. Take a hoe, sir—take a hoe, and stand to your defense this instant!

Rodney

Don't make a scene!

Duke

Rodney, you are an egregious ass! Take a hoe—do you hear me, sir?

Bush

Pull up the weeds, Jacob—and lay down a bit v'morl along the sparrow grass.

(aside)

Lock her in, d'yer hear? Lock her in and lose the key!

Duke

Lock her in, d'you say? You villainous ruffian! So, you've trapped some other wretched creature into your clutches. Can't even stand by your partner in crime. I dare say that house is positively swarming with degraded females at this very moment.

(Van Adam and Mrs. Verulam abruptly disappear from their window.)

Rodney

I scarcely think the house is swarming—

Duke

I am not addressing myself to you. I have nothing to say to you. My business is with this gentleman. Stop digging this moment, or I shall not wait for you to fight. I shall kill you without further parley!

Jacob

Where d'ye wish it laid?

Bush

Along the sparrow grass, I tell yer. Then, get to mulching.

Duke

Marl and Mulching be damned!

(presenting hoe)

Rodney (to Bush)

Save yourself.

(Bush backs off.)

Duke

Rodney, how dare you interfere?

Rodney

Duke, I am your second. Fight if you must, but fight like a man. Don't murder a man in his bean sprouts.

Duke (wildly)

I'll murder him where I choose. Will you be killed or will you fight?

Bush

I won't be killed.

Duke

Then, stop mulching, and get your second to come out on the grass—and we'll have it out fairly.

Bush

Jacob, Jacob—

Jacob

What der yer want?

Bush

Give over, Jacob.

Duke

Take your hoe and follow me.

Mrs. Verulam (appearing at the window)

What are they doing? Why is the Duke so angry?

Van Adam

I expect Mr. Bush is going to show him how to hoe the garden.

Mrs. Verulam

Well, but what's the Duke doing now? He's measuring the ground with a pocket handkerchief.

Van Adam

No, how am I going to change my trousers?

Duke

Come on, nothing will save you!

Duchess (feebly, from the mushroom house)

Help! Help! Murder! Murder!

Rodney

Whatever's that?

Duke

I know that voice.

Duchess

Help, help!

Jacob

An innercent lady in the mushroom house.

Duke

In there! An innocent lady in such a hole as that!

(pushing by Bush and going to the mushroom house)

You scoundrel! It's locked! It's bolted! Where's the key? Rodney, why don't you fetch the key?

Rodney

Because I don't know where it is.

Duke

And you call yourself a man. She'll be dead in another minute.

Rodney

Try your hoe, Duke, try your hoe.

Duke

By Jove, I will.

(breaking open the door)

CLEOPATRA!

(The Duke turns towards Bush with murder in his eye. Bush drops his hoe and runs towards the house. Enter the Bun Emperor, accompanied by Mr. Harrison and Bliggins.)

Harrison

Here's your man, oh, most certainly, by all means.

Emperor

Arrest him! Arrest him!

Duke

Let me kill him! Let me kill the scoundrel!

Emperor

Not till I've skinned him for stealing my property.

Rodney

For heaven's sake, don't make a scene before the ladies.

Harrison

Rely on me, oh, indeed, most certainly, in all circumstances, rely on me.

Jacob

The innercent lady—she ain't stifled.

Duchess

Yes, I am an innocent lady. Oh, Southborough! He wouldn't

speak for me, he fled, the base one fled. He's not a man.

(Enter Mrs. Van Adam.)

Van Adam

No more am I.

Mrs. Verulam (protesting)

Chloe!

Van Adam

It's all over, Daisy. We couldn't keep this up forever.

Rodney

The gentleman's a lady?

Duchess

This man, a woman? But then, you are, you are—

Mrs. Verulam

Respectable!

Duchess

Then, I shall have to send Lady Pearl to Carlsbad this summer. Unless Mr. Ingerstall—Southborough, come away.

Mrs. Verulam (to the Emperor)

Now, you must release Mr. Bush: this is all a mistake.

Emperor

Let him go, Mr. Harrison. Let the ruffian go!

Harrison

Rely on me, sir.

Emperor

We do, Mr. Harrison, we do.

(Bush, released, goes back to his hoeing.)

Mrs. Verulam

Mr. Bush, goodbye.

(Bush continues to hoe.)

Duke

Goodbye, Mr. Bush.

Bush

Get on with yer!

(Mrs. Verulam turns away and takes Rodney's arm.)

Rodney

You will not leave society.

Mrs. Verulam

Perhaps—perhaps not! I must think. I must ponder.

Marriner (coming up)

Ma'am, may I speak?

Mrs. Verulam

Certainly, Marriner. What is it?

Marriner

With your permission, ma'am. I desire to enter into matrimony.

Mrs. Verulam

Indeed! With whom?

Marriner

Mr. Harrison.

Mrs. Verulam

Oh.

Marriner

I feel that I can rely on him, ma'am.

CURTAIN

THE GREEN CARNATION

CAST OF CHARACTERS

Betty, Lady Windsor, a hostess about forty years of age

Emily, Lady Locke, her widowed cousin, about twenty-eight years of age

Esmé Amarinth, a wit, writer, and dandy, in his forties

Lord Reggie Hamilton, a dandy and follower of Mr. Amarinth

SCENE I

A drawing room in a country house, circa 1894.

A late Victorian drawing room in an English country house not far from London. Lady Windsor and her cousin, Lady Emily Locke, enter, throwing off their cloaks.

Emily

It's been a delightful evening.

Lady Windsor

Do you think so? I thought you would like Lord Reggie.

Emily

I meant the music.

Lady Windsor

Oh, Faust is always nice.

Emily

I think it's a mercy something stands still nowadays. London is not the same London it was ten years ago, when I left.

Lady Windsor

I should hope not. Why, Aubrey Beardsley and Mr. Amarinth had not been invented then—one never heard of Ibsen and Shaw—and women hardly ever smoked, and—

Emily

—and men did not wear green carnations.

Lady Windsor

You act as if you dislike our times. Do you really object to the Green Carnation?

Emily

I'm not sure. Is it some sort of secret sign? Everyone who wore it revolved around Mr. Amarinth like satellites around the sun.

Lady Windsor

They wear it to be original and to draw attention to themselves.

Emily

By their dress? I thought that was the prerogative of women?

Lady Windsor

Oh, but men have women's minds, just as women have men's minds, these days. It's the modern thing to do.

Emily

I hope not. Has Lord Reggie got a woman's mind?

Lady Windsor

Oh, he's absolutely fearless.

Emily

That's better.

Lady Windsor

For example, if he wanted to do something absolutely depraved, he would do it shamelessly.

Emily

He's not afraid to be wicked?

Lady Windsor

Oh, no indeed. Not in the least. How many of us can say as much? Do you like Lord Reggie?

Emily

He has a beautiful face. How old is he? Twenty?

Lady Windsor

Oh, nearly twenty-five. Three years younger than you are.

Emily

He looks astonishingly young.

Lady Windsor

Oh, yes. He says his sins improve his complexion.

Emily

Did he say that, or Mr. Amarinth?

Lady Windsor

Mr. Amarinth said it first, I believe. But, about Lord Reggie?

Emily

Then, pretty Lord Reggie is just a copycat.

Lady Windsor

Oh, no—he's marvelous in his own right.

Emily

Who started the fashion of the Green Carnation?

Lady Windsor

That was Mr. Amarinth's idea. He wears it because it blends with the color of absinthe.

Emily

It sounds rather silly to me. They must be dyed.

Lady Windsor

Of course. That's why they are so original. Nature will soon begin to imitate them. However, she has not started yet.

Emily

That is lazy of her. (back to the subject of Lord Reggie) Has he a mother?

Lady Windsor

Who?

Emily

Lord Reggie.

Lady Windsor

Oh, he has two.

Emily

Two?

Lady Windsor

Practically. His own mother divorced his father, who is a perfectly horrid man. And his father's second wife wrote him a letter the other day, saying she was prepared to be a mother to him. So you see, he has two.

Emily

Do you know her?

Lady Windsor

No. Nobody does. But I believe she is very tall and religious—if you notice, it is generally short squat people who are atheists—and they say she does a great deal of good among the rich. She has actually converted some to Christianity, and you know, that's very hard.

Emily (pondering)

Then, she is a good woman?

Lady Windsor

Lord Reggie is very fond of her. He spent a day with her last year, and he was so pleased with her that he's planning to do it again this summer. He's even going to introduce her to Mr. Amarinth, and he wouldn't do that unless he thought very highly of her.

Emily

Do you believe in Mr. Amarinth?

Lady Windsor

Oh, certainly. He gives one ideas and that is very convenient. People who keep cudgeling their brains for ideas are always so stupid. Mr. Amarinth gives you enough ideas for a week, at least.

Emily

I suppose he gives Lord Reggie all his thoughts?

Lady Windsor

Oh, he supplies half London. Hush, I think Lord Reggie and Mr. Amarinth are coming now.

(Enter Lord Reginald Hamilton and Mr. Amarinth. Both wear Green Carnations, and both affect extravagant fashions.)

Reggie (bowing)

We simply couldn't go to bed without telling you how much we enjoyed the evening.

Emily

The opera was magnificent.

Amarinth

I wonder they don't have morning opera—from twelve to three; one could have breakfast at eleven and arrange a lunch party between the acts.

Emily

Oh, but one would be fit for nothing afterwards.

Amarinth

Quite so. How beautiful! Half London thoroughly unfitted for any duties whatever. It makes me so uneasy to meet with people doing their duty. I find them everywhere. It is impossible to escape them. Duty destroys the mind. In fact, it is fatal to all higher feelings.

Emily

Now, you are laughing at me, Mr. Amarinth.

Lady Windsor

Oh, no, Emily. Mr. Amarinth never laughs at anyone. He makes others laugh.

Amarinth

Humor moves me to tears. There is nothing so utterly pathetic as a really fine paradox. Truth—is always inappropriate.

Reggie

Exactly, Esmé. That is why I laughed at my mother's funeral. Anybody can cry. I forced my grief beyond tears.

Emily

Surely people were shocked?

Amarinth

When are they not shocked?

Reggie

They said I was heartless. But, one cannot choose carefully with deliberation. Deliberation is fatal to one's personality. When I am what is called wicked, it is my mood to be evil. I never know what I shall be at a particular time. There are moments when I desire squalor.

Lady Windsor (uneasily)

Yes, moods are delightful. I have as many as I have dresses, and they cost me nearly as much. They cost my husband a good deal—but fortunately, he can afford them. But I never go slumming. There are so many microbes there. I can't imagine why microbes flourish in the slums—nothing else does. And so, a mood that cost me typhoid or smallpox would be really silly, wouldn't it? Will you excuse us? I want to show Emily something. Come,

Emily

(Exit Lady Windsor and Emily.)

Amarinth (after they have gone)

How tiring women are. They always let one know they are up to the mark. Isn't it so, Reggie?

Reggie

Yes—unless they have convictions. Lady Locke has convictions, I fancy.

Amarinth

Probably. But, she has a great deal besides.

Reggie

How's that?

Amarinth

Don't you know why Lady Windsor especially wanted you here

tonight?

Reggie

To polish your wit with mine?

Amarinth

No, Reggie. Lady Locke has come into an immense fortune lately. Lady Windsor is trying to do you a good turn.

Reggie

Hmmm.

Amarinth

It's a pity I am already married. I am paying for my matrimonial mood now.

Reggie

But, I thought your wife only lived on potted meats and stale bread?

Amarinth

Unfortunately, that is only a canard invented by my dearest enemies. What do you think about it, Reggie? Could you commit the madness of matrimony with Lady Emily Locke? You are so wonderful as you are, so complete in yourself, that I scarcely dare wish it. You live so comfortably on debts, that it might be unwise to risk the possible discomfort of having money. Still, if you ever intend to possess it, you had better not waste time.

Reggie

Do you know my theory of money?

Amarinth

No. What is it, Reggie?

Reggie

I believe that money is gradually becoming extinct. It is vanishing off the face of the earth like the dodo. Soon, we shall have people saying that money was seen at Richmond, like the Loch Ness Monster, or that a bird watcher heard two capitalists singing in the woods near Esher. One hears that money is tight, a most vulgar condition for money to be in, by the way. Do you want money?

Amarinth

I suppose I do—but I am afraid of spoiling myself.

Reggie

Marriage hasn't changed you.

Amarinth

Because I have not let it. My wife began by trying to influence me—and has ended by being influenced by me. She is a good woman, Reggie—and wears large hats. Why do good women wear large hats? Someone told me the other day that the Narcissus Club had failed because it did not go on paying. Nothing does go on paying. I know I don't.

Reggie

I hate paying anyone, even when I have the money. There is something so sordid about it. To give is beautiful. I said as much to my tailor yesterday. He had the impertinence to reply, "I differ from you, sir, in toto." How horrible the spread of education is.

Amarinth

It will spoil England if it continues. It has already spoiled America. People say we are so wicked, Reggie. I wish I could feel wicked. Only saints feel wicked, they're always repenting. It must be delightful. It's the only reason I can think of for putting up with the inconveniences of sanctity. The stars are so unjust.

Reggie

Are you going to get drunk tonight, Esmé? You're so splendid when you are drunk.

Amarinth

Don't know yet. Never do. To get drunk deliberately is as foolish as to get sober by accident. Reggie, are you going to make this marriage?

Reggie

Do you want me to?

Amarinth

I never want anyone to do anything. But, I should be delighted no longer to pay for your suppers. But marriage might make you develop, and then I should lose you. Don't develop, Reggie. Whatever you do, don't develop. The secret of my success is that I never develop. I was born epigrammatic and I shall die with a paradox on my lips. Do not marry unless you have the strength to resist orthodoxy and be a bad husband.

Reggie

I have no intention of being a good one.

Amarinth

When you marry, you make vows—and nothing is so damaging to personality as keeping promises. To lie finely is an art. To tell the truth is to act according to nature. Nothing on earth is so absolutely middle class as nature.

Reggie

Only people without brains make good husbands.

Amarinth

Lady Locke would make a good wife.

Reggie

Yes. It is written on her face. The worst virtues are those that cannot be concealed.

Amarinth

Yes—we can conceal our vices, if we like, for a time, at least. But virtue will out.

Reggie

Oh, Esmé, when you are drunk, I could listen to you forever.

Amarinth

Remember my epigrams, dear boy, and repeat them to me tomorrow. I am dining out with Oscar Wilde, and that is to be done only with prayer and fasting. It is not easy to be wicked. To sin beautifully, as you sin, Reggie, is one of the most complicated of the arts. There are hardly six people in a century who can master it. To commit a perfect sin, Reggie, is to be great. The works of man perish. But what sin that has ever been invented has been demolished? There are always new human beings springing into the world to commit it, to find pleasure in it.

Reggie (ecstatically)

Esmé, you are great.

Amarinth

How true that is. In conceit lies salvation. We do not hoodwink ourselves into modesty.

Reggie

Hsst. The ladies are coming back.

(Emily and Lady Windsor return with some food.)

Lady Windsor

Have some buns, everyone. Lord Reggie? They are so wholesome.

Reggie

Wholesome things almost always disagree with me. If I ate one,

I should almost infallibly lose my temper.

Amarinth

Curious! My temper and my heart are the only two things I never lose. Losing things is a very subtle art. Almost anybody can find things. So few people can lose anything really beautifully.

Lady Windsor

I wish I could find some money. Times are so very hard for the rich, don't you think so? I shall soon have to give up my carriage, or your brother. I can't keep them both up.

Amarinth

Poor Teddy! Have his conversational powers fallen off?

Lady Windsor

Oh, no, he still talks rather well. He is a superb raconteur—I shall miss him much.

Emily

The profession of conversationalist is so delightful. I wonder more people don't take it up.

Reggie

The true artist will always be an amateur.

Lady Windsor

Conversational powers are sometimes so distressing.

Emily

At least I have none. Otherwise, I should be quite hopeless. Like Mr. George Bernard Shaw—

Lady Windsor

Oh, he means well.

Amarinth

I am afraid so. People who mean well always do badly. Good intentions are invariably ungrammatical.

Reggie

Good intentions have been the ruin of the world. I have no intentions.

Emily

Then you will never marry.

Amarinth

To be intentional is to be middle class. It is quite mistaken to think the artist should stuff his beautiful empty mind with knowledge of any kind. I have written a great novel on Iceland—yet, I couldn't find the place on the map. I only know that it has a beautiful name, and I have written a beautiful book about it. Like a seacoast in Bohemia. This is an age of identification in which our God is the Encyclopaedia Britannica.

Reggie

These strawberries are good. I should finish them, only I hate to finish anything. Finishing things is so commonplace. It is more original not to.

Emily

You are very fond of originality?

Reggie

Are not you?

Emily

Oh, no. I've lived among soldiers.

Reggie

Soldiers are never original. They think it unmanly. They know nothing about anything or anybody—which would be charming—only they think they know everything.

Emily

You must have been unfortunate in your experiences.

Reggie

Perhaps so. I tried to be manly. I talked about Kipling and Conrad, which is a sure sign of manliness—but, they only wanted to talk about machine guns and horses.

Emily

You have finished the strawberries after all.

Reggie

So I have. We, none of us, live up to our ideals. Nothing is so limited as to have an ideal.

Emily

But, you look as though you have many.

Reggie

Oh, never believe what you see in a person's face. Faces are only masks given us to conceal our thoughts. No more preposterous thing has ever been put forward than that of the artist revealing himself in his art.

Lady Windsor

Mr. Smith, the curate, is coming tomorrow. You must remember to be very high church.

Reggie

I don't know how to be high church. How does one do it?

Lady Windsor

Oh, just abuse the evangelists. There is nothing to it.

Reggie

If I were anything, I would be a Roman Catholic.

Emily

Would you like to confess your sins?

Reggie

Immensely. There's nothing so much fun as telling people about your wickedness. Curiously enough, good people love hearing it. Strange. Sinners take absolutely no interest in good people.

Amarinth

Society loves one thing more than sinning.

Emily

What is it?

Amarinth

Administering injustice.

Emily

I am sure Lord Reggie has a great deal of good in him.

Amarinth

Not enough to spoil his charm. You know, I was reading the Bible recently. I had no idea it was so artistically written. There are passages in the book of Job that I should not be ashamed to have penned myself.

Emily

I wonder if authors know how dangerous they may be in their writing.

Amarinth

One has to choose between being dangerous and being dull.

Emily

But, some books have made suicide quite the rage. Take Hedda Gabler, for instance.

Reggie

True. A number of most respectable ladies, without the vestige of a past among them, have put an end to themselves lately. To die naturally has become quite unfashionable.

Amarinth

No doubt the tide will turn presently.

Lady Windsor

I suppose Ibsen and Shaw are responsible for a good deal.

BLACKOUT

SCENE II

When the lights go up, it is sometime the next day. The drawing room is occupied only by Mr. Amarinth, who is in a somewhat languishing attitude. Emily enters.

Emily

Why, what's the matter, Mr. Amarinth?

Amarinth

Ah, Lady Locke. I was just contemplating the vanity of life. Why have I never set the world ablaze? I have plied the bellows most industriously, and I have made the twigs crackle, and yet, the fire splutters a good deal. You have a beautiful soul, and I have a beautiful soul. Why should there not be a sympathy between us?

Emily

Some circumstances have been unkind to you, perhaps?

Amarinth

That could not hurt me—for I am no philosopher, and never take facts seriously.

Emily

Are you a pessimist?

Amarinth

I hope so. Optimism destroys the soul. Nothing is so unattractive as goodness except, perhaps, a sane mind in a sane body. To believe is very dull. To doubt is intensely engrossing. People become pessimists to save themselves from intellectual annihilation.

Emily

Your notions are very odd.

Amarinth

Let me put it to you another way. Could you love a man you felt you could understand?

Emily

Certainly. Especially if he were difficult for others to understand.

Amarinth

The moment we understand a human being, our love spreads his wings—preparatory to flying away.

Emily

You go very far in your admirable desire to amuse.

Amarinth

I think not. Doubt and jealousy fan affection into passion. Women used to understand this—but now, men are waking up from their slumber and becoming inscrutable. Lord Reggie is an example of what I mean.

Emily (guardedly)

Lord Reggie is very unusual.

Amarinth

Lord Reggie is unlike everything except himself. He would make any woman unhappy. How beautiful.

Emily (irritated)

Is it always a sign of intelligence to be what others are not?

Amarinth

Dear lady! Intelligence is the demon of our age. Mine bores me horribly. I am always trying to find remedies for it. I have experimented with absinthe, but I gained no result. I have read the collected works of Karl Marx. They are said to sap the mental powers. They did not sap mine. Cocaine has proved useless—and leaves me positively brilliant. What am I to do?

(Enter Lord Reggie.)

Reggie

What is that about intelligence?

Emily (leaving)

Unfortunate man! You should treat your complaint with the knife. Become a popular author. (she is gone)

Reggie

What ails her?

Amarinth

Reggie, Lady Locke will marry you, if you ask her.

Reggie

I suppose so.

Amarinth

Will you ask her?

Reggie

I suppose so.

Amarinth

Have a carnation, yours is wilting.

(Reggie takes a new carnation from Amarinth, and fixes it in his buttonhole.)

Amarinth

So, you are to be a capitalist, Reggie? Will you warble in the woods near Esher? Will you flute to the great god whom stockbrokers worship so vulgarly? Vulgarity has become so common, it has lost all its charm. I shall really not be surprised if good manners come into vogue again.

Reggie

You are marvelous, Esmé. You are like a scent in the air. You make people aware of you who have never seen you, never read you.

Amarinth

What shall I give you for a wedding present, Reggie?

Reggie

Esmé, what do people do before they propose? There must be some absurd way to lead up to it? I can't just whistle at her. I'm sure she will expect something.

Amarinth

My dear Reggie, women always expect something. They are like the sons of the nobility. They live on their expectations.

Reggie

What am I to do? I really can't just put my arm around her waist. One owes something to oneself.

Amarinth

One owes everything to oneself. I also owe a great deal to other people, which I hope I shall not live long enough to repay.

Reggie

But, how shall I propose my proposal? How did you do it?

Amarinth

I did nothing. My wife proposed to me, and I refused her. Then, she put up something called the banns, and told me to meet her at a certain church on a certain day. I declined. Would you believe, she came to fetch me? To avoid a scene, I went with her. Voilà tout.

Reggie

I must trust my intuition then?

Amarinth

I'd rather you trusted your emotions.

Reggie

But, I have none for Lady Locke. How could you suppose so?

Amarinth

It is the privilege of incompetence to suppose. The artist will always know. Go to Lady Locke, and tell her that you do not love her, and will marry her. That is what a true woman loves to hear.

Reggie

Are the creatures so perverse?

Amarinth

It's the secret of their charm. I believe she is coming back. I shall vanish. (Amarinth exits quickly)

Emily

I'm sorry, I was rude in leaving so quickly.

Reggie

You seem to have frightened Mr. Amarinth off.

Emily (regarding his carnation)

How do you manage to keep that flower alive so long?

Reggie

I don't understand.

Emily

Why, you've worn it two days.

Reggie

This? No, Esmé and I have some sent down every morning from a florist's in Covent Garden.

Emily (surprised)

Really! Is it worthwhile?

Reggie

I think it's the only sort of thing that is worthwhile. I worship little details. Let others worship what they call great things.

Emily

Is it an emblem?

Reggie

Certainly not. I wouldn't have such a thing about. I hate mementos. I prefer to forget things. There is nothing more beautiful than to forget, except, perhaps, to be forgotten.

Emily

Then, why do you wear it?

Reggie

Because it is beautiful. Isn't that reason enough?

Emily

But, the color is not natural.

Reggie

Not yet. Nature has not followed art so far. Nature requires time.

Emily

Nature is going to quite a vulgar extreme today. It is decidedly too hot.

Reggie

Esmé invented this flower two months ago. Only a few wear it.

Emily

Who?

Reggie

Those who are followers of a higher philosophy.

Emily

What is that?

Reggie

To be afraid of nothing. To dare to do as one wishes—to have the courage of one's desires.

Emily

Mr. Amarinth is the high priest of this philosophy, I suppose?

Reggie

Esmé is the bravest man I know. He sins more perfectly than I do. He escapes those absurd things, consequences. His sin always finds him out. He is never at home to it by choice. Why do you look at me so strangely?

Emily

Do I look at your strangely? Perhaps, it's because you are so unlike the men I'm accustomed to. Your aims are so different.

Reggie

That is impossible, Lady Locke.

Emily

Why?

Reggie

Because I have no aims. I have only emotions.

Emily

Are you one of those who make a god of their temperament?

Reggie

Temperament should guide one's life, of course.

Emily

The blind leading the blind.

Reggie

It's beautiful to be blind. Those who can see are always avoiding the things that would give them the most pleasure. Esmé says that to know how to be led is a much greater art than to know how to lead.

Emily

I don't care to hear the epigrams and opinions of Mr. Amarinth. His epigrams are his life. If he were silent, he would die.

Reggie

You're not being fair. He's going to give a speech to some school children. Will you hear it?

Emily

I suppose so.

Reggie

You don't know him at all, really.

Emily

And you know him far too well.

Reggie

You sound just like my father.

BLACKOUT

SCENE III

When the lights go up, Amarinth is standing on an improvised podium or pulpit. Lady Windsor, Emily, and Lord Reggie are seated. If possible, there should be some children listening, too.

Amarinth

Dearly beloved. I have come before you to speak of the art of folly. That is to say, the art of being foolishly beautiful. The art has been practiced in all ages, among all peoples, from the pale dawn of creation, to the golden noontide of this century. Always, throughout the circling ages, man has, to some slight extent, aspired to folly, as Nature strives to imitate art. We are only beginning, only beginning, to understand the beautiful art of folly. But the mind of man has stubbornly clung to fallacies that have greatly interfered with the sublime progress of folly.

To give only a few instances. For century upon century, we have been told that children should obey their parents, that the old should direct the young, and that Nature is the mother of beauty. Men have stopped up their ears to the alluring cries of folly—have gone to their graves with all their sublime absurdities still in them, unuttered, repressed. Folly has been trampled by the swinish majority.

(Lord Reggie has been giving signs of enthusiasm throughout this portion of Esmé's speech. Emily has listened with increasing uneasiness. Lady Windsor has applauded whenever she thought her social duty required it.)

Amarinth

But, at last there seems to be a prospect of better things—the flush of a wonderful dawn in a hitherto shadowy sky. I believe, I dare to believe, that a bright era of undisciplined folly is about to dawn over the modern world.

Therefore, my children, recognize your exquisite potentiality for foolishness. Wisdom has had its day. The stars are beginning to twinkle in the violet skies of folly. It is not given to all of us to be properly foolish. The ill effects of heredity are to be seen everywhere. Even the influence of myself, of Lord Reginald, of Oscar Wilde, and of a few, a very few, others has so far failed to root up the pestilent plant of wisdom from the retentive soil of humanity. Many still (looking at Emily) are content with the old virtues, still timorous of new vices. To know how to disobey is to know how to live. It has hitherto been the privilege of age to rule the world. In the blessed era of folly, that privilege will be transferred to youth. It is very difficult to be young, especially up to the age of thirty—and very difficult to be foolish at any age at all. But, we must not despair. I am absurd. For years I have tried in vain to hide it. But, I am not without hope. My absurdity is, at last, beginning to win me a measure of recognition. A few, a divine few, are beginning to understand that absurdity. "What is absurdity, but the perfection of folly?" has a glorious future before it. I have brought the art of preposterous conversation to perfection. But, I have been greatly handicapped in my efforts by the folly of a world which persists in taking ME seriously.

Bishops declare I am a monster, and monsters declare I ought to be a bishop. All this, because I was born to be absurd. Because I have lived to be absurd. I married to be absurd. I shall die to be absurd. Someday, the exquisite art of folly will take its place with painting, music, and literature. Strike the words virtue and wickedness from your dictionaries. There is nothing good, nothing evil. Despise the normal. Shrink from nature. Remember, folly is true wisdom. Amen. Go to French plays; they will do you so much harm. May the god of foolishness bless you all the days of your life.

(Enthusiastic response from everyone except Emily, who sits rigid and furious.)

BLACKOUT

SCENE IV

When the lights go up, we are back in the drawing room. Emily and Lord Reggie enter in a tête-à-tête.

Emily

What a blessing a short memory can be.

Reggie

Didn't you like the lecture, then? I thought it splendid—so full of imagination, so exquisitely choice in language and feeling.

Emily

And, so contrived and self-conscious.

Reggie

As all art must be.

Emily

Art! Art! You almost make me hate that word.

Reggie (shocked)

You could hate art?

Emily

Yes. If it is the antagonist of nature— No, I did not like the lecture, it was absurd. Tell me, Lord Reggie, are you self-consciously absurd?

Reggie

I hardly know. I hope I am beautiful. To be beautiful is to be complete. That is all I wish for. Esmé said today that marriage was a brilliant absurdity. Will you be brilliantly absurd? Will you marry me?

Emily (after a pause and with deep feeling)

I cannot marry you. I am not brilliant, and therefore, have no wish to be absurd. You don't love me. I think you love nothing. I might fall in love with you, but I can never love an echo—and you are an echo.

Reggie

An echo is often more beautiful than the voice it repeats.

Emily (furiously)

Not if the voice is ugly. You imitate Mr. Amarinth. I believe he merely poses, although what he is, is quite impossible to say. Do you merely pose? Who are you, really? Are you what I see?

Reggie

Expression is my life.

Emily

Then, what I see is you?

Reggie

I suppose so.

Emily

Then, never ask a woman to marry you. Men like you do not understand women. If you took that hideous green obscenity out of your coat—not because I asked you—but, because you genuinely hated it, I might give you a different answer. I want a natural flower to wear over my heart. Are you angry with me?

Reggie (peeved)

You talk like an ordinary person.

Emily

I am ordinary. I think, in the future, I shall try to be more ordinary than I already am. Someday, perhaps, you will throw away that green carnation.

Reggie (lightly)

Oh, it will be out of fashion soon.

(Emily turns on her heel and walks away. After a moment Amarinth walks in.)

Amarinth

So, you have been refused, Reggie. How original you are. I should never have expected that of you. When did you decide to be refused? You managed it exquisitely. Ah, Reggie. You will not be singing in the woods near Esher.

Reggie, give me a gold-tipped cigarette, and I will be brilliant. I will be brilliant for you, as I have never been brilliant for my publishers. I will talk as no character in my plays has ever talked. Let me be brilliant, dear boy, or I shall weep for sheer wittiness, and die as so many have died, with all my epigrams still in me. Come.

(Lord Reggie and Mr. Amarinth go out, arm in arm, as the curtain falls.)

CURTAIN

ABOUT THE AUTHOR

Frank J. Morlock has written and translated many plays since retiring from the legal profession in 1992. His translations have also appeared on Project Gutenberg, the Alexandre Dumas Père web page, Literature in the Age of Napoléon, Infinite Artistries.com, and Munsey's (formerly Blackmask). In 2006 he received an award from the North American Jules Verne Society for his translations of Verne's plays. He lives and works in México.

www.ingramcontent.com/pod-product-compliance
Lightning Source LLC
LaVergne TN
LVHW041615070426
835507LV00008B/244